PENGUIN BOOKS

JADE LIPTON

cakestar

YOUR GUIDE TO CREATING SHOW-STOPPING CAKES

PENGUIN BOOKS
Published by the Penguin Group
Penguin Group (NZ), 67 Apollo Drive, Rosedale,
Auckland 0632, New Zealand (a division of Pearson New Zealand Ltd)
Penguin Group (USA) Inc., 375 Hudson Street,
New York, New York 10014, USA
Penguin Group (Canada), 90 Eglinton Avenue East, Suite 700, Toronto,
Ontario, M4P 2Y3, Canada (a division of Pearson Penguin Canada Inc.)
Penguin Books Ltd, 80 Strand, London, WC2R 0RL, England
Penguin Ireland, 25 St Stephen's Green,
Dublin 2, Ireland (a division of Penguin Books Ltd)
Penguin Group (Australia), 250 Camberwell Road, Camberwell,
Victoria 3124, Australia (a division of Pearson Australia Group Pty Ltd)
Penguin Books India Pvt Ltd, 11, Community Centre,
Panchsheel Park, New Delhi – 110 017, India
Penguin Books (South Africa) (Pty) Ltd, 24 Sturdee Avenue,
Rosebank, Johannesburg 2196, South Africa

Penguin Books Ltd, Registered Offices: 80 Strand, London, WC2R 0RL, England

First published by Penguin Group (NZ), 2012
3 5 7 9 10 8 6 4 2

Copyright © Jade Lipton, 2012

The right of Jade Lipton to be identified as the author of this work in terms of
section 96 of the Copyright Act 1994 is hereby asserted.

Designed and typeset by Sarah Healey, © Penguin Group (NZ)
Photography by Paul Giggle
Prepress by Image Centre, Ltd.
Printed in China by South China Printing Company

All rights reserved. Without limiting the rights under copyright reserved above,
no part of this publication may be reproduced, stored in or introduced into a retrieval
system, or transmitted, in any form or by any means (electronic, mechanical,
photocopying, recording or otherwise), without the prior written permission of
both the copyright owner and the above publisher of this book.

ISBN 978 0 14356581 9

A catalogue record for this book is available
from the National Library of New Zealand.

www.penguin.co.nz

contents

Acknowledgements 5
Introduction 6
Equipment 9
Edible Decorations 11

Icings 12
Baking Basics 16
Essential Skills 19
Cake Designs 25

Templates 136
Index 142

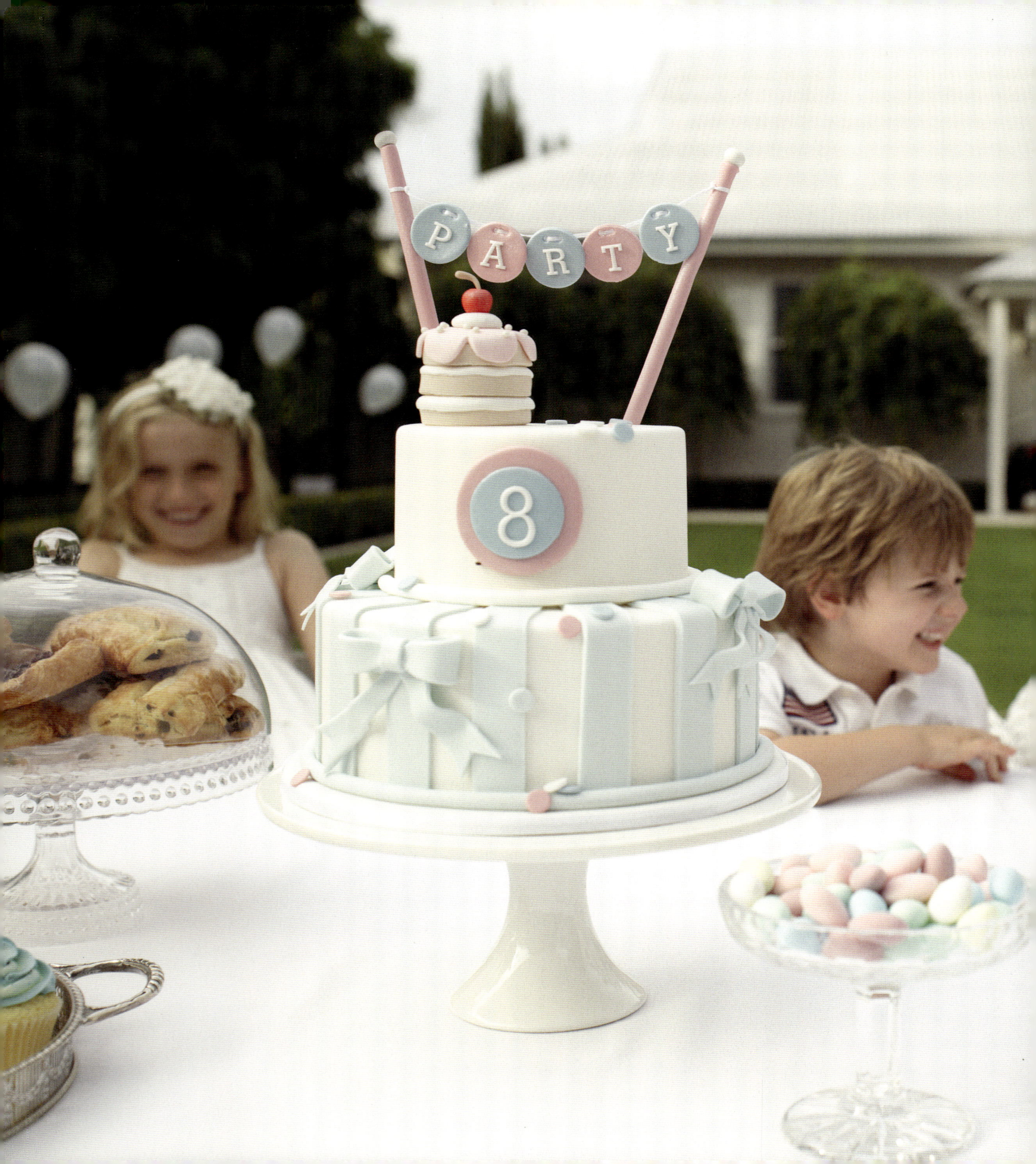
PARTY
8

For Mia & Finnley

Special thanks to

The Batchellor family for opening their home to us for the photography of this book; Mamma's Home for use of their beautiful props; Emma, Catherine and Sarah at Penguin; Dean and Julie for their friendship and opportunities; and to Bakels Australia and Queen for their sponsorship, which allowed me to make this book as visually delicious as the cakes inside it.

BAKELS

QUEEN EST 1897

introduction

I could think of no more perfect name than CakeStar for my little store full of talented decorators, as our cakes have a reputation for being the star attraction at any event – shining bright among clients who include celebrities, royalty, fashion designers, sports stars and more.

Young or old, woman or man, when a beautifully decorated cake ablaze with candles is placed in front of you, the reaction is so wonderfully, genuinely happy, appreciative and heartfelt. A cake is a gift of your time, skills and thought that will become the centrepiece of the occasion, a talking point for months to come immortalised in photographs and a precious memory for life. This is how my love affair with cake decorating began and I hope this book will inspire you to make this rewarding art form a part of your life, too.

secrets to success

The first secret I would like to share with you is this: cake decorating is not difficult!

The home baker *can* easily create the show-stopping cakes, cupcakes and biscuits in this book and even make their own versions by adapting the designs, using very little equipment and with little experience.

The second secret is that being a 'creative' type is not essential – you will actually find that organisation is far more important.

The planning, preparation, recipes, techniques and step-by-step instructions in this book will be your introductory course to becoming a capable cake decorator. It is definitely worthwhile reading the earlier chapters of this book before embarking on creating any of the designs.

planning

Even with professionals, a cake is normally constructed over at least three days. Sometimes, if masses of handmade flowers or sculpted figures are to be made, they are started weeks before the finished cake is due. The more work you can do ahead, the less chance you will be a tired wreck when it comes to party time.

For freshness, cupcakes are best baked and decorated in one day. Larger cakes can of course be baked, cooled and decorated quickly; however, for maximum results and minimal stress, follow these rules:

At least one week ahead of time: Read through all recipes and decorating instructions. Make sure you have all the items you require. With the rise in popularity of cake decorating, most kitchenware stores have a section dedicated to decorating equipment; however, some equipment may need to come from a specialist store, or you could buy it online.

Three days before: Bake and cool your cakes (wrap firmly in plastic wrap once cool) and make up any icings. Cakes can be too soft to decorate on the day they are baked, and modelling fondant and ganache need to sit overnight to be easily worked with.

Two days before: Layer, sculpt and cover the cake with ganache. Make any decorations that need to be dried ahead of time. The ganache will need to set firmly so you have a firm base to work with and can achieve sharp edges and a neat finish when covering with fondant.

D-Day – Decorating Day: Cover your cake in fondant, decorate and, most importantly, have fun!

your workspace

I grew up in the country and learned from women who made the most beautiful cakes in the most dilapidated farm kitchens. You really just need a clean, smooth work surface, such as a table or bench top, and a sink for washing your hands and equipment – you will find that you are constantly washing your hands to avoid sticky fingers and marks on your cake. White hand towels are advisable – if you dry your hands on coloured hand towels, coloured fibres are sure to sneak their way into your icing.

Make sure you keep all other cooking away from your cake area – while you are decorating your cake, that part of the kitchen is a no-go zone, as a splash of water will eat holes in your icing and food could cause contamination.

People can get caught up in the decorating of their cake and forget it is actually a food that will be eaten by party guests. This is a very hands-on process, so be mindful of good food hygiene.

Have all your requirements easily accessible – you don't want to have a bubble in your icing and take 10 minutes to find a pin to burst it, for example.

storing your completed cake

Heat, humidity and sunlight can break down the icing, causing it to soften and lose shape, and the colours to fade or run. Place your cake, cupcakes or biscuits in a sturdy box and store in a cool, dry area away from direct sunlight. Never store your cake in the refrigerator.

cakestar 8

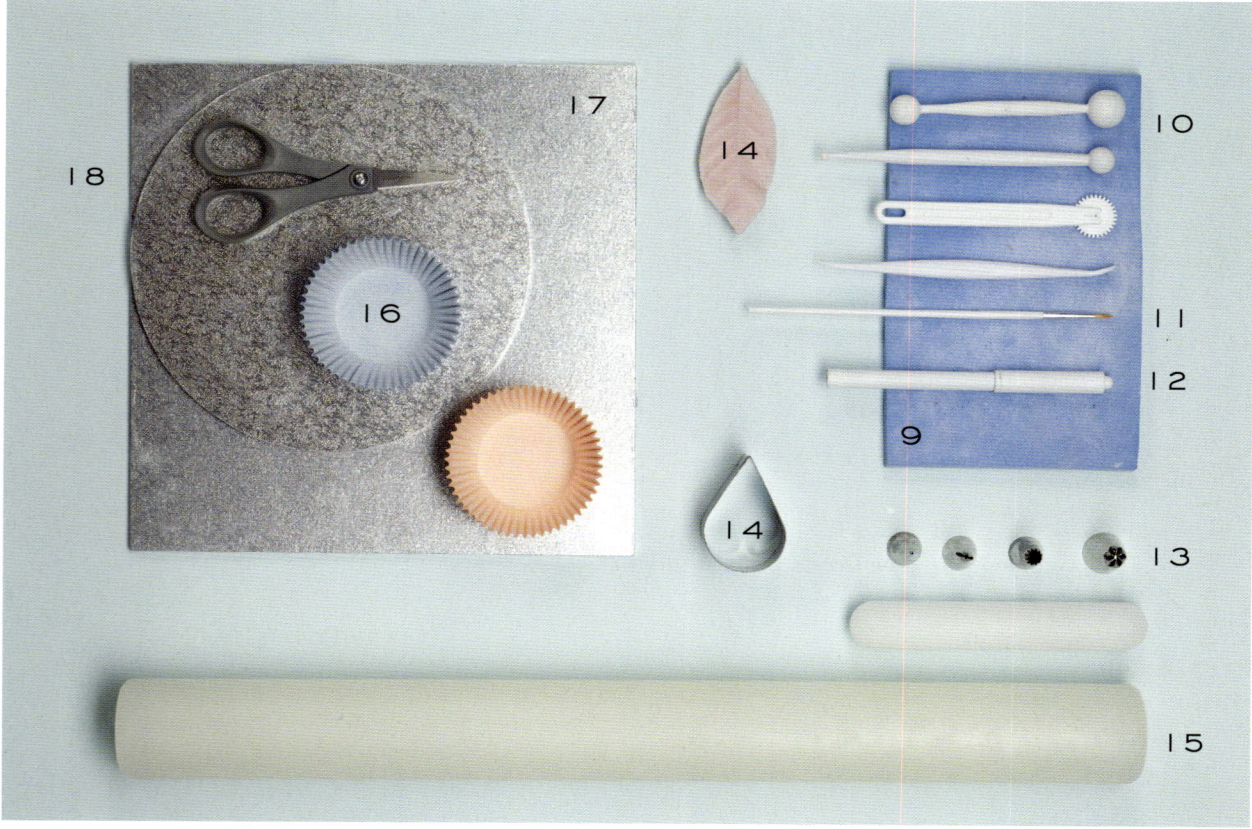

equipment

There is no end to the amount of equipment that can be bought for cake decorating; a professional cake decorator's kit can cost thousands of dollars. The cakes in this book have been designed to require minimal equipment, often making use of household items. As a cake decorator, you will become quite inventive, beginning to look at all manner of things as a possible tool, something that could emboss a pattern into your icing or support a modelled item as it dries.

1. **Large and small palette knives:** For coating cakes in ganache and buttercream. They are also ideal for lifting decorations into position.
2. **Various metal and plastic cutters:** Endless shapes and sizes are available. Pictured are metal and plastic flower cutters for use with modelling fondant, metal square cutters that can be used with fondant and to cut shapes from biscuit dough and lettering cutters for use with fondant.
3. **Knives:** A small sharp pointed knife is essential for cutting shapes, trimming icing and marking designs. A large serrated knife is best for cutting and shaping cakes.
4. **Supports:** Often added support is needed when creating more elaborate designs. Pictured are lollypop sticks, decorator's wire and thick wooden skewers. Be sure to make people aware if these non-edible items are in the cake you create.
5. **Non-stick work board:** Makes rolling and cutting small shapes from fondant much easier.
6. **Icing smoothers (pair):** For a perfect finish to fondant icing.
7. **Straight-edged scraper:** For achieving neat straight edges when coating cakes with ganache.
8. **Turntable:** Gives easy access to all sides of the cake, particularly useful when coating round cakes with ganache.
9. **Foam pad:** Use as a base for softening edges and cupping petals.
10. **Modelling tools:** The ball tools, stitching tool and Dresden tool are used for marking and shaping fondant.
11. **Artist's paintbrushes:** A selection from fine to quite broad. Soft is ideal for dusting.
12. **Food-colouring pen:** To write and make precise markings on fondant.
13. **Various piping tips:** For use with a coupler and piping bag to pipe royal icing or for cutting small rounds.
14. **Leaf veiner and leaf cutter:** Embosses veins to create realistic leaves. Flower veiners are also available.
15. **Large and small rolling pins:** The larger rolling pin is useful for rolling out icing to cover cakes and is an essential part of your decorating kit, while the small rolling pin is useful for smaller and more intricate tasks.
16. **Cupcake cases:** Available in many sizes, colours and patterns. Be sure that you buy cupcake cases that fit your cupcake trays.
17. **Cake boards:** Used as a base for your cake or to separate tiers, they are available in all manner of shapes and sizes. They can come in thick cardboard, but more ideal are those made from masonite and covered in silver or gold food-safe paper.
18. **Scissors:** For cutting templates and trimming icing and ribbons.

3
9
4
2
6
7
8
PME
ARTS &
Crafts
PEARL
CHEFMASTER
7306 ROYAL BLUE
GEL COAL BLACK
Wilton
Sprinkles
Yellow Sugar

edible decorations

Cake-decorating supply stores and even supermarkets stock a huge variety of edible decorations that not only add an extra touch to your cake, but also save on time. For a shortcut, use the Queen Icing Flowers on the Petit Tiered Cakes (see page 41), or fish lollies instead of the handmade sea creatures on the Cupcake Aquariums (see page 100). When catering for a large number of guests, you may even mix and match elaborately decorated cupcake designs from this book with some simply iced cupcakes that are dressed up with sparkly Queen Cachous, chocolate hearts or sugar confetti. For added impact, spray your creations with edible lustre to make them shine.

essential decorations

1. **Chocolate curls.**
2. **Cachous:** Sugar cachous or dragées come in different sizes, colours and shapes.
3. **Spray lustre:** An aerosol can of edible pearl lustre that can easily be applied to most types of icing.
4. **Paste food colours:** More concentrated than liquid food colours, these work best with fondant icing, while liquid colours are ideal for buttercream. Powdered colours are also available.
5. **Ready-made Queen Icing Flowers.**
6. **Edible lustres and petal dusts in a range of colours:** These can be mixed with decorator's alcohol or a clear spirit, such as vodka, to become a liquid that can be painted onto icing.
7. **Lollies and chocolates.**
8. **Sugar confetti:** Comes in many colours and shapes such as hearts, butterflies, spots, stars, Christmas trees and more.
9. **Nonpareil sugar balls:** Also known as hundreds and thousands.

cakestar 11

icings

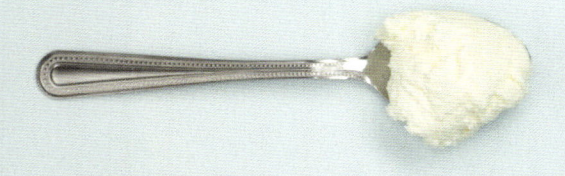

buttercream

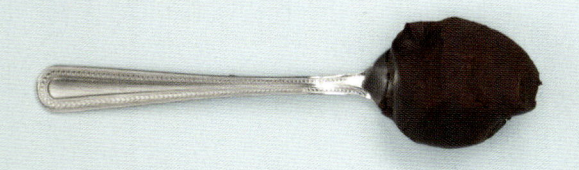

dark chocolate ganache

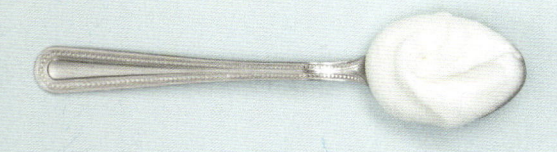

royal icing

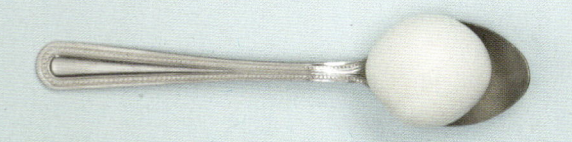

fondant

BUTTERCREAM

Every morning at CakeStar we make bowls and bowls of this simple icing. We pipe it into neat little rosettes that adorn the cupcakes in our cabinet or apply it under fondant icing on large cakes or cupcakes instead of ganache. The results are not as precise, but it is delicious and perfect for children. This buttercream is useful for white colour schemes or can be coloured using liquid or paste food colourings.

250 g butter, softened
500 g icing sugar, sifted
1 tsp vanilla extract or vanilla bean paste

1. Place butter in the bowl of an electric mixer fitted with a paddle attachment and beat until pale, almost white.
2. Turn off mixer, add icing sugar then beat until pale and fluffy.
3. Add vanilla (or flavouring of your choice) and beat until combined.

FLAVOURING SUGGESTIONS

Essences: Replace vanilla with essences of strawberry, coffee or even peppermint. Add a few drops at a time, to taste.
Citrus: Add finely grated zest of 1 lemon or orange to completed mix. Lemon or orange essence can also be used.
Chocolate: Beat in half a quantity of dark chocolate ganache (see next recipe).

DARK CHOCOLATE GANACHE

Dark chocolate ganache is a decadent mixture of boiled cream and chocolate. A delicious base coat of ganache is the secret to a perfectly iced cake, concealing any imperfections to give a smooth surface, neat edges and a stable base to cover with fondant icing. Our cakes have to be able to withstand high temperatures during the summer, so our ganache recipe has a high ratio of chocolate to cream. If in a cooler climate, use a little more cream so your ganache doesn't set too quickly. Ganache can be stored in the refrigerator for up to 1 week.

1 kg dark chocolate (preferably couverture), buttons or block broken into pieces
440 ml cream

1. Place chocolate in a heatproof bowl.
2. Heat cream to just boiling and pour over chocolate. Allow to stand for 2 minutes, then stir with a whisk to combine. Stand a further 2 minutes then whisk again.
3. Cover bowl of ganache with plastic wrap and leave to sit at room temperature overnight before use.

MICROWAVE METHOD

Place chocolate in a microwave-safe bowl and pour cream over. Microwave on high power for 1–2 minutes. Remove from the microwave, stir, then return to the microwave for another minute, stirring again afterwards. Repeat until ganache is smooth.

ROYAL ICING

Royal icing is an essential for any decorator to master. It sets extremely hard, making it perfect for putting together the layers of tiered cakes and securing decorations on an iced cake. Correctly made royal icing with a soft-peak consistency is perfect for piping borders, decorations and messages on cakes while a stiff-peak consistency can be used for piping raised flowers and so on. Royal icing sets very quickly if left open to the air. If you are not using your icing immediately, ensure it is covered with plastic wrap or a crust will form. Instant royal icing is available in supermarkets but it is very simple to make your own.

1 egg white
250 g pure icing sugar, finely sieved
1 tsp lemon juice

1. Ensure all utensils are clean and dry.
2. Place egg white in a bowl and whisk lightly with a dessertspoon to break up.
3. Add icing sugar a spoonful at a time, mixing well after each addition, until you are happy with the consistency – for piping you will need a soft-peak consistency, as pictured.
4. Add lemon juice and mix again, adding a little more icing sugar if consistency becomes too soft.
5. Cover with plastic wrap until ready to use. Royal Icing keeps for up to 1 week in a cool dry place; refrigeration is not recommended.

TIPS FOR ROYAL ICING

Use only pure icing sugar, not icing mixture, and ensure the eggs are at room temperature, never directly from the refrigerator, as the consistency of the icing will change as the cold egg white warms. All egg whites have a different mass, so the amount of icing sugar required varies a little; just add the icing sugar a spoonful at a time until you are happy with the consistency. A super-fine sieve can be bought from specialist cake-decorating stores and produces royal icing that is far better to work with.

FONDANT ICING

Fondant or RTR (Ready-to-Roll) icing is one of the few food products I will ever say you are better to buy ready made rather than make your own. To achieve the quality finishes of the cakes in this book, you must use good-quality fondant. There are many brands on the market, some readily available in supermarkets. Each brand will have its own characteristics. After 10 years of experience and having tried many, many brands, we use Bakels Pettinice RTR Icing in our store every day and it was used for every cake in this book. You will find it referred to as fondant icing in the instructions for each cake. It is easy to work with, covers cakes beautifully, colours well, has a great texture and finish, and with the addition of tylose powder is fantastic for modelling. In Australia, Bakels Pettinice is generally only available in specialty cake-decorating stores in 7 kg quantities; however, smaller retail packs are sold in some New Zealand supermarkets.

Adding tylose powder to fondant icing to make a quick modelling fondant.

TIPS FOR STORING FONDANT

If you are only able to buy a large quantity of fondant, bear in mind that it generally keeps for up to 12 months if stored correctly in a cool, dry place (check the manufacturer's instructions and best-before date). Keep the fondant completely sealed, removing as much air as possible from the packaging to prevent it drying out and forming a crust.

QUICK MODELLING FONDANT

There are many recipes for modelling pastes that make hard-drying figures and flower pastes for fine, china-like sugar flowers. However, the novelty designs in this book can all be easily achieved using fondant and sometimes, for a little extra strength and to speed up the drying and setting process, we add tylose powder to create a quick modelling fondant.

1 tsp tylose powder to every 100 g fondant

1. Knead fondant until soft and pliable. Make a small indent in the centre, place in tylose powder, fold icing over to envelop powder and knead until evenly combined in the fondant.
2. Wrap tightly in plastic wrap and store in a cool, dry place. Modelling fondant is best if left to sit overnight before use; however, it can be used immediately.

If modelling fondant becomes too hard or cracks easily when being worked with, knead in a small amount of extra fondant. If still too soft, add more tylose powder.

TYLOSE POWDER

Tylose powder or CMC (carboxymethyl cellulose) gum is available in cake-decorating stores and online. It is a food-safe powdered gum that when added to fondant icing helps it to set hard, often combating the effects of humidity on the icing in our climate. We also combine tylose powder with water to make edible glue.

DECORATOR'S GLUE OR TYLOSE GLUE

While some decorators just use water, we combine tylose powder with water to create an edible glue to assemble decorations, attach decorations to cakes and to adhere icing to cake boards. A small artist's paintbrush is perfect to apply tylose glue exactly where it is needed. If glue is too thick, add a little extra boiled cooled water.

¼ tsp tylose powder
60 ml boiled and cooled water

1. Add tylose powder to water and stir. Allow to sit until dissolved and the mix becomes a clear gel (around 10 minutes).
2. Use immediately or store covered in the refrigerator until needed (for up to 1 week).

APRICOT GLAZE

This glaze is brushed over cakes coated with ganache directly before covering them with fondant. It allows the fondant to stick to the set ganache.

50 ml water
40 g apricot jam

1. Boil water and pour over apricot jam in a small heatproof bowl, then whisk with a fork to combine.
2. Strain through a sieve to remove any lumps.
3. Use immediately or store in the refrigerator until needed (for up to 1 week).

baking basics

These are our two most popular and versatile recipes, giving you a deliciously moist cake that is easy to work with and stays fresh for up to a week. We use these two base recipes to create up to 30 different flavour combinations. Try our suggestions or experiment with your own ideas. The quantities can be safely reduced for smaller batches or multiplied for larger batches.

Each recipe makes enough mix for one 23-cm (9") round cake or around 24 medium cupcakes. You will find that when baking some of the cakes in this book, you will have a little mix left over; use this to experiment with different flavour combinations in cupcakes.

WHITE CHOCOLATE & VANILLA CAKE OR CUPCAKES

This recipe makes a beautiful vanilla cake with true home-baked flavour. The white chocolate acts to extend the freshness of the cake, but has a very mild flavour, making this recipe perfect for children and adults alike.

1⅓ cups plain flour
1 cup self-raising flour
250 g butter, softened
150 g white chocolate, broken into pieces
2 cups caster sugar
300 ml full-cream milk
2 eggs, lightly beaten
1 tsp vanilla extract (we use Queen vanilla bean paste)

1. Preheat oven to 160°C (150°C fan forced) and prepare cupcake trays or cake tins (see opposite). Sift flours into a bowl and set aside.
2. Fill a medium-sized saucepan to a third full with water and bring to a gentle simmer. Put butter and white chocolate in a heatproof bowl and place over saucepan, ensuring base of bowl does not touch simmering water. Stir occasionally until butter and chocolate have melted.
3. Add caster sugar and milk to chocolate mixture, mixing gently with a hand whisk over gentle heat until the sugar is completely dissolved.
4. Remove bowl from saucepan and mix in sifted flours in three lots, ensuring there are no lumps of flour.
5. Whisk in eggs and vanilla extract or flavouring of your choice (see below).
6. If you are filling cupcake cases transfer mix to a jug. Fill cake tin or cupcake cases to two-thirds full.
7. Bake until a skewer inserted in centre of the cake comes out clean. Test after 1 hour 20 minutes for a 23-cm (9") round cake and around 20 minutes for cupcakes.
8. Leave large cakes to cool completely in the tin for several hours or overnight. Leave cupcakes for 5 minutes, then remove from the tray and place on a wire rack to cool completely.

FLAVOURING SUGGESTIONS

The first three are recommended for the white chocolate and vanilla recipe and the next three for the double chocolate recipe.

Citrus: Add finely grated zest of 1 lemon or orange. Lemon or orange essence can also be used.
Raspberry: Swirl (but don't completely mix through) ⅓ cup crushed raspberries through finished mix.
Caramel: Caramel oil can be bought from specialist stores. Add a small amount to taste.
Mocha: Add 3 tsp coffee essence.
Hazelnut: Replace ⅓ cup plain flour with hazelnut meal. Add ¼ cup hazelnut liqueur.
Rum and Raisin: Soak ⅓ cup raisins in ¼ cup rum overnight, then add to mix.

DOUBLE CHOCOLATE CAKE OR CUPCAKES

The alcohol in this recipe keeps your cake fresh for much longer. While you may notice a slight taste of port and sherry, the alcohol content evaporates during cooking.

1⅓ cups plain flour
1⅓ cups self-raising flour
⅔ cup cocoa
300 g butter, softened
180 g dark chocolate, broken into pieces
2 tbsp granulated instant coffee
300 ml hot water
2½ cups caster sugar
⅔ cup port
⅔ cup sherry
2 eggs

1. Preheat oven to 160°C (150°C fan forced) and prepare cupcake tray or cake tin.
2. Sift flours and cocoa together into a bowl and set aside.
3. Fill a saucepan to a third full with water and bring to a gentle simmer. Put butter and dark chocolate in a heatproof bowl and place over saucepan, ensuring base of bowl does not touch simmering water. Stir occasionally until butter and chocolate have melted.
4. Dissolve coffee granules in the hot water and add to chocolate mixture along with caster sugar, mixing gently with a hand whisk over gentle heat until sugar is completely dissolved.
5. Remove bowl from heat and whisk in port and sherry.
6. Whisk in sifted dry ingredients in three lots, ensuring there are no lumps of flour remaining, then whisk in eggs. Mix in flavouring of your choice (see opposite).
7. If you are filling cupcake cases, transfer mix to a jug. Fill cake tin or cupcake cases to two-thirds full.
8. Bake until a skewer inserted in the centre of cake comes out clean. Cooking times will vary greatly depending on the size and depth of the cake you are baking. Test after 1 hour 30 minutes for a 23-cm (9") round cake and around 20 minutes for cupcakes.
9. Leave large cakes to cool completely in the tin for several hours or overnight. Leave cupcakes for 5 minutes, then remove from the tray and place on a wire rack to cool completely.

PREPARING CAKE TINS

Cupcake trays: Cupcake cases and trays come in many sizes. Be sure to check that your cases fit the tray you will be using. To line cupcake trays, simply place a single cupcake case in each cup.

Standard cake tins: Use good-quality non-stick baking paper. To line the sides of your tin, measure the distance around the tin and add a little extra to allow for an overlap where the paper will join. Cut a strip of baking paper to this length and to a width 4 cm greater than the height of the tin. Make a 2-cm-wide fold along the length of the strip that will fold down into the base of your cake tin and, if lining a round tin, make cuts along the folded section at 2-cm intervals to allow it to curve into position. Place the tin on baking paper and draw around it, cut out the shape just inside the lines and this piece will line the base of your cake tin. Spray the tin with non-stick baking spray, line the sides first and then the base.

Ball and rounded tins: Spray the tin or bowl thoroughly with non-stick baking spray, put a small round of baking paper in the base, then dust the inside of the tin lightly with flour. Many glass and metal mixing bowls are oven-safe and can be used in place of ball tins.

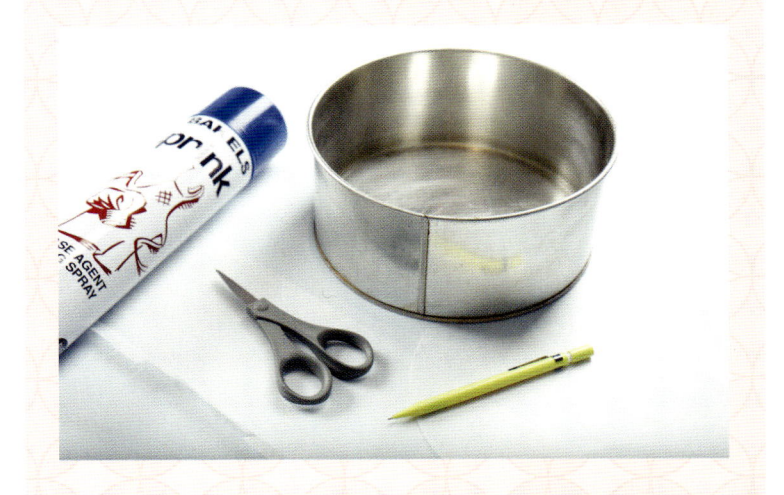

VANILLA BEAN BISCUITS

These biscuits keep their shape well when baking and stay fresh for up to 2 weeks when stored in an airtight container. You can use vanilla essence, but I love the speckled effect of vanilla seeds through them so use fresh vanilla bean seeds or vanilla bean paste.

250 g butter, softened
1 cup caster sugar
1 tsp vanilla bean paste or seeds of 1 vanilla bean
1 egg
2 cups plain flour

1. Place butter, sugar and vanilla (or any flavouring you wish to use) in bowl of an electric mixer and, using paddle attachment, beat until creamy and pale.
2. Add egg, beating until well incorporated.
3. With mixer turned off, add flour then mix on low speed until just combined. Scrape sides of the bowl then mix again briefly.
4. Use your hands to form the dough into a flat disk, wrap in plastic wrap and refrigerate for at least 1 hour before use.
5. Grease a baking tray and line with non-stick baking paper.
6. Knead dough briefly on a lightly floured work surface then roll out between 2 sheets of baking paper to an even thickness of 5 mm.
7. Remove top sheet of baking paper and use templates and a sharp knife or biscuit cutters to cut out your biscuits. Transfer to prepared baking tray using a palette knife and place in the refrigerator to rest for 30 minutes. Offcuts can be re-rolled and used.
8. Preheat oven to 170°C (160°C fan forced).
9. Bake until lightly browned at the edges. Baking time will vary greatly depending on size of biscuits. Small biscuits take around 8 minutes, while larger ones, such as the walls of the Vanilla Bean Birdhouse (see page 130), take around 17 minutes.
10. Allow baked biscuits to rest on the tray for 5 minutes before transferring to a wire rack to cool completely.

FLAVOURING SUGGESTIONS

Lemon: Add finely grated zest of 1 lemon to the mixture. Lemon essence can also be used.
Chocolate: Replace ⅓ cup plain flour with sifted cocoa.

essential skills

I am constantly asked how we get our cakes to look so perfect. The secret is all in the application of the ganache and first layer of fondant icing. Cakes and cupcakes must always be completely cooled and larger cakes are best to rest for a day before preparation.

LEVELLING CAKES

1. To level the cake, with the 'crusted' side of your cake facing up, use a ruler and cocktail sticks to mark an even height around the cake.
2. Use a large serrated knife to trim the top from the cake, the cocktail sticks acting as a guide. Set the top aside.
3. Remove the cocktail sticks.

While very soft fillings or fillings that require refrigeration are not suitable when the cake is to be iced with fondant, for added flavour and visual impact when you cut and serve the cake, you can cut one or more horizontal layers into your levelled cake and sandwich these together with ganache. To do this, mark even layers around the cake using the previous technique and cut the cake into the desired number of layers.

COVERING A CAKE WITH GANACHE

Ganache is best to use when soft, but not too liquid. If it is too runny it will not cover and spread correctly; if it is too hard, it will cause the sides of your cake to crumble as you try to spread it. If the ganache sets too hard, it can be softened by gently warming in the microwave.

What had been the top of your cake while baking (and has now had the crust removed) will become the bottom of your cake and the base will become the top so you have the neatest and most crumb-free surface possible to work with for decoration. Use ganache to secure the cake to the cake board.

1. If you are filling the cake with ganache, spread it generously with a palette knife before sandwiching on the next layers. Make sure you place the cake layers on top of each other neatly, so you maintain straight sides and a level top.
2. Coat the sides of your cake first. Use a palette knife to apply more ganache than necessary, as you are better to use more and scrape off the excess for a neat finish. By coating the sides first, you are able to use your hand on top of the cake for control.
3. Cover the top of the cake in an even layer of ganache.
4. Working quickly, use a straight-edged scraper to neaten the sides of the cake. When covering square or rectangular cakes with ganache, take extra care on the corners, using your straight-edged scraper to get sharp edges. When covering rounded cakes with ganache, a straight-edged scraper is not suitable for the top. Instead use a piece of flexible cardboard that can curve into shape.
5. Use the straight-edged scraper to smooth and neaten the top of the cake, taking care to form neat edges.
6. If possible, allow the cake to sit overnight to set before icing.

COVERING A CAKE WITH FONDANT

Brush the cake with a thin, even coating of apricot glaze (see page 15). This will be the adhesive between the set ganache and the layer of fondant. Wipe the cake board with a clean, damp cloth to remove any ganache or apricot glaze that could mark your icing.

1. Dust a work surface with a little sifted pure icing sugar. Cut fondant into manageable pieces and knead until soft and pliable. Combine pieces and knead into one smooth, flattened ball.
2. Dust a work surface with cornflour and use a large rolling pin to roll out fondant, lifting it slightly and turning fondant 45 degrees after every few rolls until it is an even thickness of around 3–5 mm and is large enough to cover the top and sides of your cake (it may pay to measure this distance with a measuring tape or string if you are not confident estimating visually). Rub surface with a smoother to polish and even icing further.
3. Carefully slide your hands and forearms under icing and lift it over cake, lowering it, starting at one side of the cake and working across. Smooth top of the cake as you go, pushing out air bubbles.
4. Smooth icing over top edges of cake and work downwards, pulling out folds of icing and smoothing with the palm of your hand.
5. Use icing smoothers to ensure icing is well adhered to the cake on the top and sides.
6. Trim excess icing away from the base of cake using a sharp knife.
7. Use two icing smoothers, one on the side of the cake and one on the top, pressed gently together to create a neat edge to the cake. The same technique is used for the side edges of square and rectangular cakes.
8. Remove any blemishes straight away. Air bubbles can be pricked with a pin and the air pushed out with careful smoothing.

The visibility of any minor cracking can be reduced by rubbing carefully with the palm of your hand. The heat from your hands will help the icing to soften and you can use smoothers to neaten further. Hide large cracks with strategically placed decorations, or concealed by filling with colour-matched royal icing.

When kneading fondant icing, you should use pure icing sugar, as cornflour tends to dry out the icing. However, cornflour is better to use on your work surface than icing sugar when rolling out fondant, as it is finer and more effective in stopping the icing from sticking to the surface. I like to keep cornflour in a little shaker bottle.

COVERING A ROUNDED CAKE WITH FONDANT

Rounded cakes are by far the easiest to cover. Follow the instructions for covering a cake with fondant icing. Smooth any straight sides with an icing smoother, but use the palm of your hand to smooth the curved areas (see photographs page 72).

ICING THE CAKE BOARD

Icing the cake board is not essential, but does add a nice finishing touch to any cake and gives a great surface to write a birthday message. There are three ways of icing the board: it can be brushed with tylose glue and covered in a large, thin piece of fondant icing, trimmed to size and the decorated cake sat on top (the decorated cake would have to be on its own board the same size as the cake); it can be covered with royal icing using a palette knife once the cake has been decorated; or the most common method is to cut a piece of fondant icing to fit snugly over and around your cake and glue it into place.

1. Roll the fondant out as you would to cover a cake, making sure it is slightly larger than the board you are going to cover.
2. Use a template the size of your cake to cut away the section where the cake sits and remove this.
3. Carefully lift the icing over the cake and lower onto the cake board, working the icing into the correct position using a smoother, if necessary.
4. Glue the icing into place using tylose glue.
5. Smooth the icing onto the board.
6. Trim with a sharp knife and allow to harden and dry before decorating the cake further, if possible – this reduces the chance of marking the icing.
7. Use colour-coordinated ribbon to hide the edges of the board, attaching with non-toxic glue.

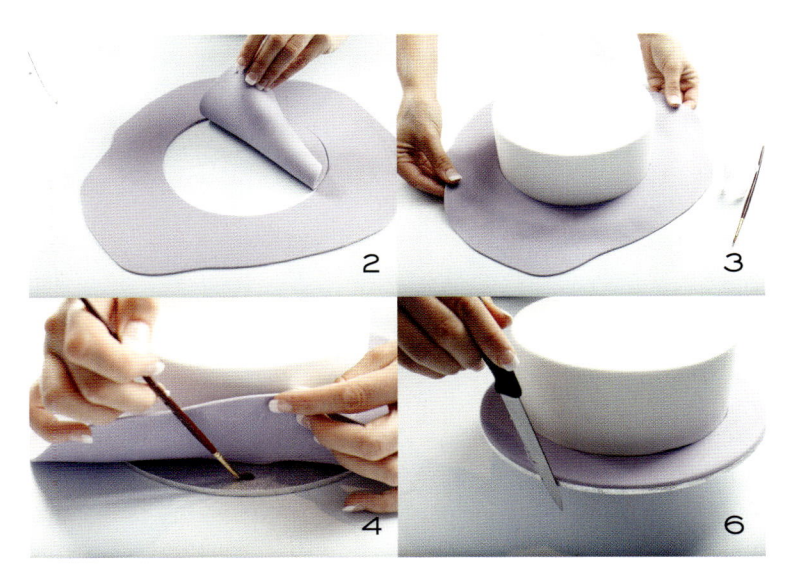

PREPARING AND ICING CUPCAKES

It is best to work on around six cupcakes at a time, covering them in buttercream, cutting fondant rounds and smoothing them, before moving on to the next six. This reduces the chance of your icing drying and cracking before the process is complete.

Levelling: The cupcake recipes in this book give a nice even surface to decorate and rarely need levelling. However, if you have had a mishap, any high spots or overflowing edges can be trimmed with a small sharp knife.

Buttercream: I find that buttercream gives a soft and forgiving surface to apply fondant icing to, concealing any little lumps and bumps that would otherwise show through the fondant. It is best to coat cupcakes in buttercream then fondant immediately as fondant will stick better to buttercream that has not yet set. With a small palette knife, place a knob of buttercream in the centre of cupcake and work outwards to give a smooth surface, being careful not to go completely to the edge so that buttercream will not show under the fondant icing.

Fondant-icing: On a surface dusted with cornflour, roll out fondant to 3–5 mm thick. Use a circle cutter slightly larger than the surface of your cupcake (this allows enough icing to cover the slightly domed surface of most cupcakes) and cut rounds of fondant. Place a round on top of each cupcake, smoothing with the palm of your hand to make sure fondant sits just inside the paper cupcake case, then use an icing smoother or paddle to get a perfect finish.

cakestar 21

FONDANT-ICING BISCUITS

I use royal icing with a soft-peak consistency to stick fondant to the surface of biscuits. If royal icing is too stiff, it will show through as raised marks on the surface of the decorated biscuit. Take care to put royal icing only where the fondant will cover, as you don't want it showing. I work on around six biscuits at a time, cutting fondant to shape, putting royal icing on the biscuits and smoothing fondant in place before starting the next six. If you work on too many biscuits at a time, the royal icing will begin to set and the fondant can dry and crack when smoothing.

1. Make up a piping bag of royal icing (see page 14) fitted with a number 2 or 3 piping tip.
2. On a surface dusted with cornflour, roll out the fondant to 3 mm thick.
3. Use same cutter or template used to shape biscuit to cut shapes from fondant with a sharp knife. Pipe an outline of royal icing just inside where edge of fondant will sit on biscuits and a little in the centre.
4. Place the fondant on the biscuits.
5. Smooth with an icing smoother or paddle to get a perfectly flat surface.

HOW TO COLOUR FONDANT ICING

Some precoloured fondants are available; however, I recommend you colour your own fondant using concentrated paste colours (with the exception of black, purely because so much colouring is required to turn white fondant black and it is such a messy process). By colouring your own fondant, you can achieve so many wonderful colours and shades, allowing you to customise the colour scheme of your cakes.

1. Use a cocktail stick to apply a small amount of paste colour to a ball of kneaded fondant.
2. Knead the colour into fondant until evenly distributed, adding more colour until the desired shade is reached. Knead in sifted pure icing sugar if fondant becomes too soft.
3. Wrap coloured fondant tightly in plastic wrap and allow to rest for at least 30 minutes or preferably overnight.

HOW TO COLOUR ROYAL ICING

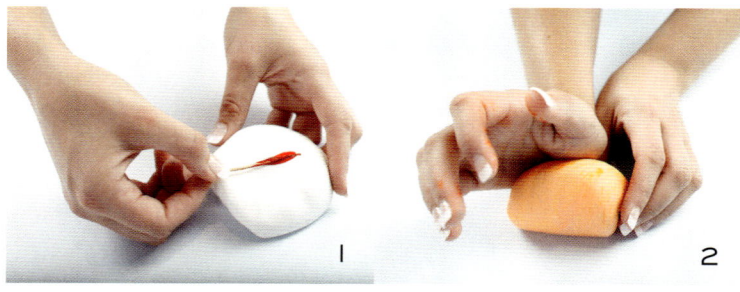

Paste, liquid or powdered food colourings can be used to colour royal icing. However, a little colour goes a long way, so start with less and build up the intensity.

1. Use a cocktail stick to apply a small amount of colour to the royal icing.
2. Mix the colour into the icing until evenly distributed, adding more colour and mixing until the desired shade is reached. Mix in a little sifted pure icing sugar if the icing becomes too runny – this is common when using liquid colours particularly.
3. Cover the icing in plastic wrap until ready to use.

Fondant icing can be softer and hard to work with when it has had a lot of colour added to it. Allow the icing to rest for a few hours after colouring, if possible; if time does not allow, a little tylose powder can be added.

PAINTING WITH FOOD COLOURS

Powdered, liquid and some paste colours can be mixed with decorator's alcohol or a clear spirit such as vodka and painted onto fondant-iced cakes. Powdered colours and lustres can be brushed on dry for a soft shading effect.

PIPING WITH ROYAL ICING

We use disposable piping bags because you can see the colour of the icing inside and the plastic keeps the icing fresh and usable longer than in nylon bags. Each piping bag is fitted with a plastic coupler that allows piping tips to be changed easily. There are many different systems available.

Filling a piping bag: Have the coupler and piping tip attached and fold the top of the bag down and over your hand (or sit the tip in a glass and fold the top of the bag over the outside of the glass) to give a good-sized opening to fill the bag and reduce the chance of getting icing all over the outside of the bag where you will later be holding it. Only half-fill the piping bag or it will be too hard to squeeze. Close the end of the bag with a rubber band to stop icing working its way out the top.

Piping is simple, but is not like writing. Follow these simple tips and practise on a plate or washable surface before piping on your cake.

- Use your dominant hand to guide the piping tip, holding it the way you would a pencil. Use the other hand further up the piping bag for support and to squeeze the icing out with even pressure.
- Always keep the tips clean – wash and dry thoroughly when switching piping tips.
- Keep piping bags wrapped in plastic while not in use to prevent the icing setting and blocking the tip. Blockages can be cleared by inserting a pin and squeezing the hardened icing out.

PIPING TECHNIQUES

Lines and writing: Hold the icing bag so it is leaning back towards you at an angle of around 45 degrees. Lightly touch the tip to the surface to 'anchor' your line, then squeeze the tube with even pressure, lifting slightly as you pull the icing towards you and allowing it to fall into position. Lower the tip and stop squeezing to end your line.

Dots and spots: With the piping bag standing straight above at 90 degrees to the surface you are decorating and just slightly above, squeeze out the icing to make a dot. You can vary the size of the dot by squeezing out more icing and lifting the tip slightly as your dot grows. If you have a raised peak, this can be flattened with a slightly damp paintbrush.

Teardrop shapes: Hold the piping bag so it is leaning back towards you at an angle of around 45 degrees. Lightly touch the piping tip to the surface to 'anchor' your teardrop, squeeze the tube to create a bulb of icing, squeezing less as you pull back to make the tail and stop squeezing to end. The shell borders you see around the bases of cakes in bakeries are simply a series of teardrop shapes joined together.

DRYING MODELLED DECORATIONS

Decorations must be allowed to set before being applied to the cake. Always place decorations on non-stick baking paper to dry, as the underside can stick to other surfaces and the decoration can break when you are trying to dislodge it. It is a good idea to sticky-tape the paper to a large square cake board so it remains a perfectly flat surface to set your decorations on.

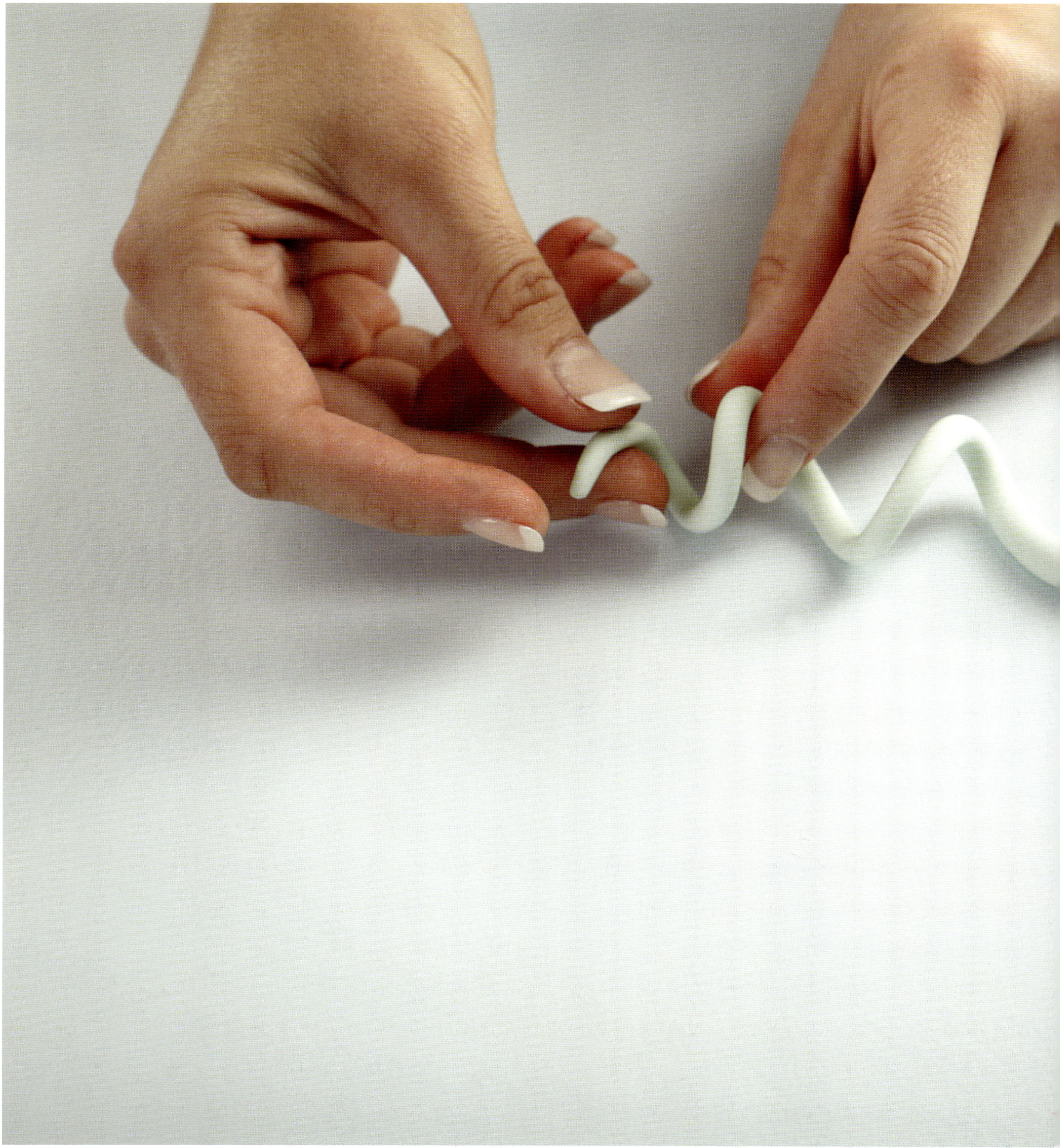

cake designs

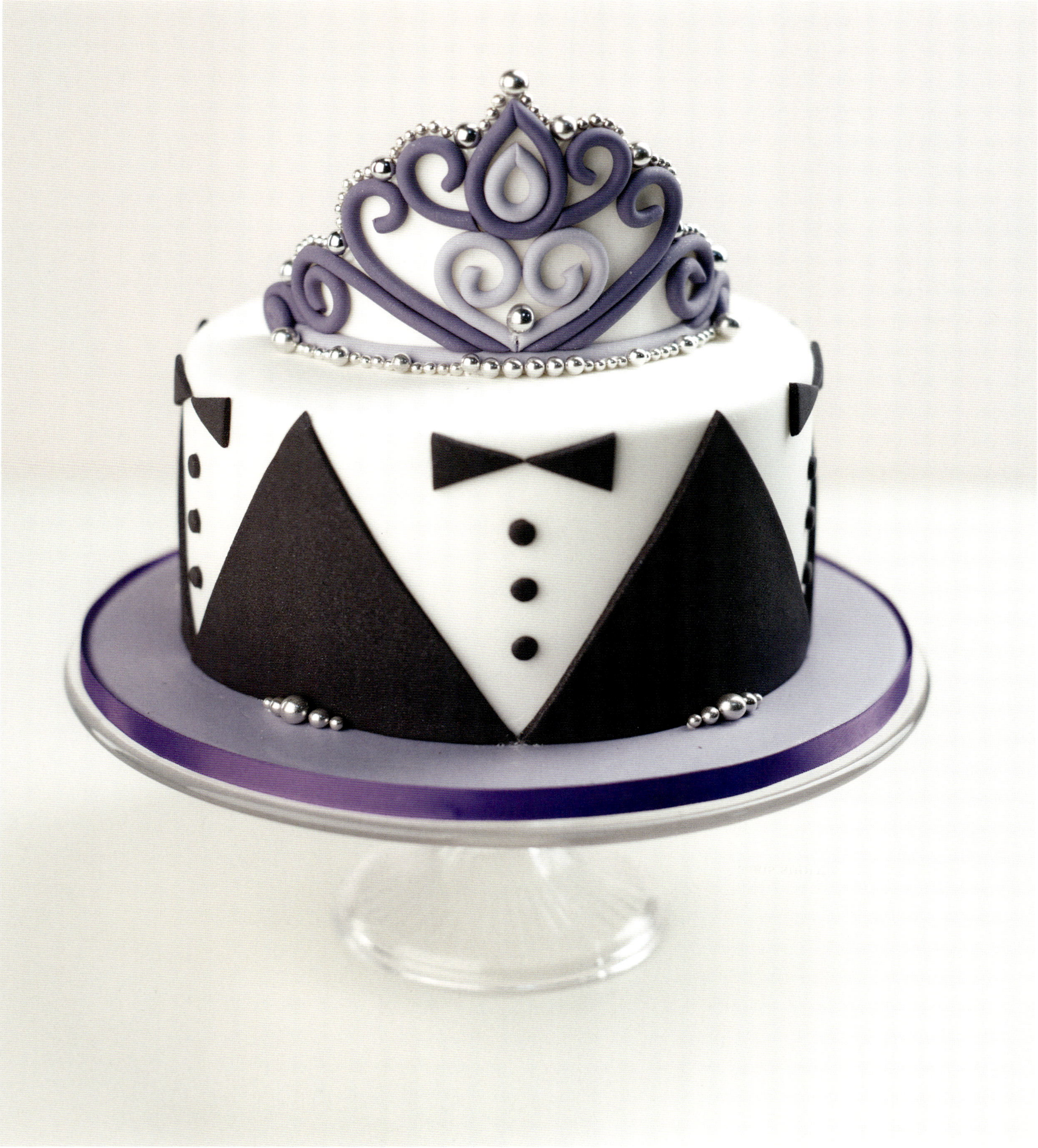

tuxedos and tiaras

Formal but fun! We get lots of requests for this cake for 18th birthday and graduation parties.

CAKE REQUIREMENTS
- 1 x 18-cm (7") round cake (see pages 16–17)

DECORATING INGREDIENTS
- 1 x ganache recipe (see page 13)
- 1 x apricot glaze recipe (see page 15)
- ½ x royal icing recipe (see page 14)
- 2.55 kg fondant icing (pre-coloured store-bought or coloured with gel paste food colouring), set aside in plastic wrap
    - 1.1 kg white
    - 800 g pale purple
    - 150 g deep purple
    - 500 g black
- pure icing sugar (for kneading)
- cornflour (for rolling out)
- tylose powder
- tylose glue (see page 15)
- silver cachous in various sizes

EQUIPMENT
- 25-cm (10") round heavy cake board
- 80 cm purple ribbon (10–15 mm wide)
- templates (see page 137)
- serrated knife
- large palette knife
- scraper with straight edge
- pastry brush
- fine sieve (for sifting icing sugar when kneading)
- large and small rolling pins
- knife
- craft knife
- smoothers
- small paintbrush (for applying tylose glue)
- number 2 piping tip
- coupler and piping bag
- number 6 piping tip (for cutting out buttons)
- non-stick baking paper (for drying decorations)
- large jar (for drying crown)
- ruler and measuring tape
- scissors
- non-toxic glue

Save time by using a store-bought tiara.

cakestar 28

STAGE ONE

1. *Prepare cake.* Level cake, removing crust from top to give a flat surface, then invert so trimmed surface becomes the base of your cake. Secure cake to the heavy board and cover with ganache (see page 19). Allow cake to set overnight, if possible.
2. *Tiara.* For best time management, tiara can be made before cake is decorated to allow maximum drying time. Knead tylose powder (see page 15) into 200 g of white fondant and roll out to a thickness of 5 mm. Use a knife or craft knife to cut around tiara template.
3. *Drying tiara.* Cover a jar or vase with non-stick baking paper, keeping in place with sticky tape if needed. Rest jar on kitchen towels if it rolls or moves. Place tiara on this to dry for several hours or overnight.
4. *Decorating tiara.* While tiara is drying it can be decorated. Roll long thin snakes of deep and pale purple, bending and cutting to shape. Lay each piece on the template as you work to make sure it is the right size, then glue in position with tylose glue.

STAGE TWO

5. *Cover cake.* Brush the cake with apricot glaze and cover using kneaded white fondant. Smooth and trim off any excess fondant.
6. *Cover board.* Knead the pale purple fondant and roll out large enough to cover the board. Cut an 18-cm (7") round from the centre, lift over the cake and onto the board, fixing with tylose glue and smoothing and trimming. Trim the edge of the cake board with ribbon, using non-toxic glue to fasten.
7. *Tuxedos.* Measure the height of your iced cake – this will be the height of each of the large triangles that form the tuxedo. Measure the distance around the outside of the cake and divide this by 5. This will give you how wide each of the 5 large triangles will be. Make your own template to these dimensions and, with a knife, cut 5 triangular pieces from black fondant rolled to a thickness of 3 mm. Use tylose glue to attach these to the side of the cake, making sure they meet neatly at the base.
8. *Buttons and bow ties.* Re-roll leftover black fondant and use the end of a round number 6 piping tip to cut 15 buttons. Cut 10 triangles using the bow tie template and a knife. Position buttons and bow ties on cake, securing in place with tylose glue.

STAGE THREE

9. *Assemble cake.* Place tiara on cake, gluing into position with tylose glue. Use white royal icing in a piping bag fitted with a number 2 tip to stick silver cachous to the tiara and cake board. Work a small section at a time so the icing doesn't dry before you have the cachous in place.

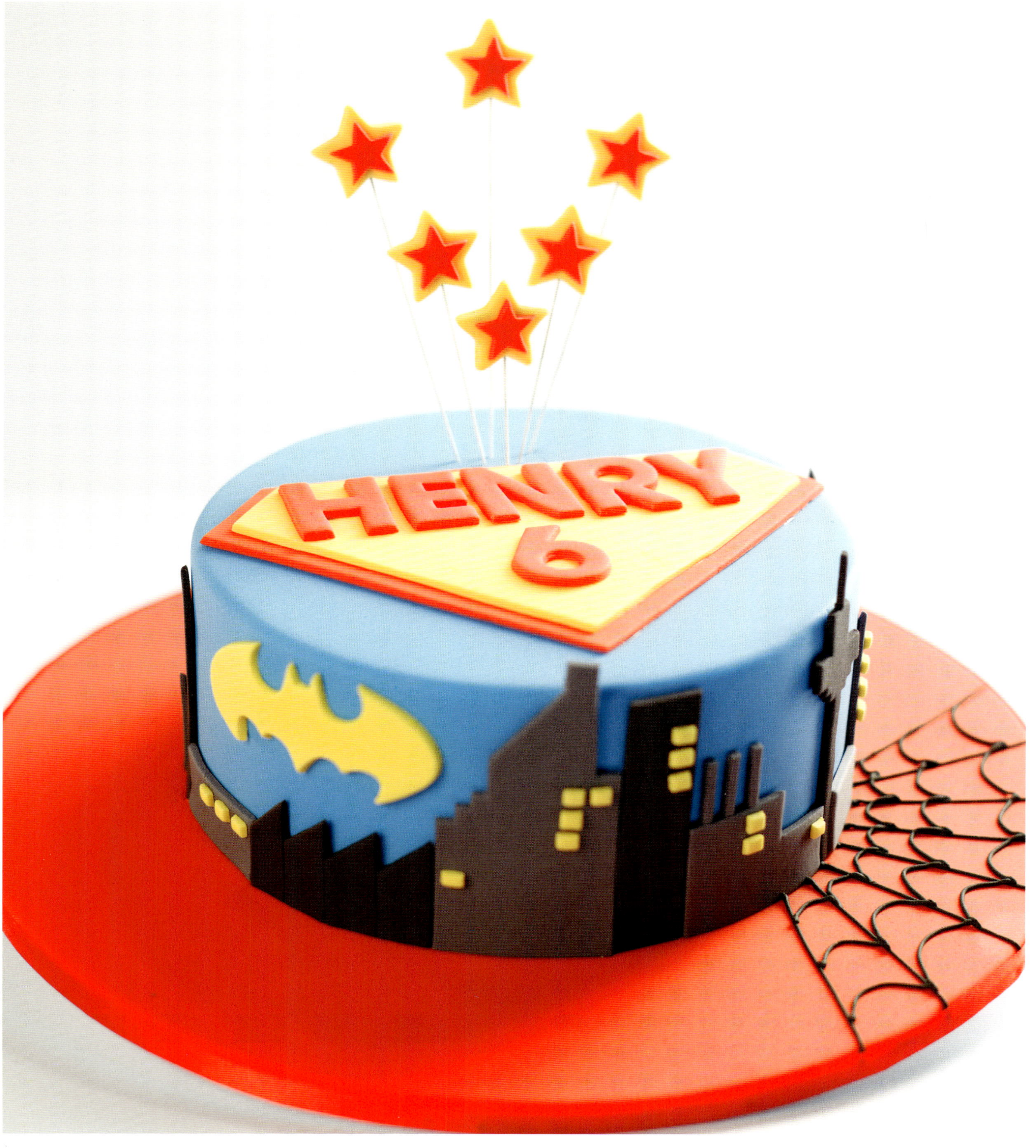
HENRY
6

hero time

Customise this super cake for comic lovers of any age by including hints to their favourite super heroes and villains.

CAKE REQUIREMENTS

- 1 x 20-cm (8") round cake (see pages 16–17)

DECORATING INGREDIENTS

- 1 x ganache recipe (see page 13)
- 1 x apricot glaze recipe (see page 15)
- ½ x royal icing recipe (see page 14)
- 2.75 kg fondant icing (pre-coloured store-bought or coloured with gel paste food colouring), set aside in plastic wrap
    - 1 kg blue
    - 1 kg red
    - 250 g yellow
    - 250 g black
    - 250 g grey
- black paste food colouring (to tint royal icing)
- pure icing sugar (for kneading)
- cornflour (for rolling out)
- tylose powder
- tylose glue (see page 15)

EQUIPMENT

- 36-cm (14") round heavy cake board
- 1.2 m red ribbon (10–15 mm wide)
- number 20 cake decorator's wires
- templates (see pages 140–141)
- serrated knife
- large palette knife
- scraper with straight edge
- pastry brush
- fine sieve for (sifting icing sugar when kneading)
- large and small rolling pins
- knife
- lettering and numeral cutters
- smoothers
- small paintbrush (for applying tylose glue)
- number 2 piping tip
- coupler and piping bag
- non-stick baking paper (for drying decorations)
- scissors
- non-toxic glue

cakestar 32

STAGE ONE

1. *Prepare cake.* Level cake, removing crust from top to give a flat surface, then invert so trimmed surface becomes the base of your cake. Secure cake to the heavy board and cover with ganache (see page 19). Allow cake to set overnight, if possible.

STAGE TWO

2. *Cover cake.* Brush cake with apricot glaze and cover using kneaded blue fondant. Smooth and trim off any excess fondant.
3. *Cover board.* Knead red fondant and roll out large enough to cover the board. Cut out a 20-cm (8") round from the centre, lift over cake and onto board, fixing with tylose glue and smoothing and trimming. Trim edge of board with ribbon, securing with non-toxic glue.
4. *Stars.* Knead tylose powder (see page 15) into yellow fondant and roll out to a thickness of 3 mm. Use a 3.5-cm star cutter to cut 6 stars. Cut 3 lengths of decorator's wire in half, dampen ends with tylose glue and insert into each star. Roll out red fondant to 3 mm thick and use a 2-cm star cutter to cut 6 red stars. Glue into position on yellow stars. Allow to dry.
5. *Name plaque.* First cut the yellow section using the name plaque template, a knife and yellow fondant rolled out to 3 mm thick. Roll out red fondant to 3 mm thick, place the yellow plaque on top of this, securing with tylose glue. Following the shape of the yellow section, cut around it so that a 1-cm border of red shows all the way around. Glue into position on top of the cake. Re-roll the remaining red fondant to 3 mm thick and use lettering and numeral cutters to cut out the name and age of the birthday child. Centre this on the yellow section of the plaque and glue in place with tylose glue when you are happy with the layout. For longer names, you may wish to use a nickname, initials or just have a large number on the plaque. If you don't have lettering and numeral cutters, you can pipe the name and age on with royal icing.
6. *City skyline and bat light.* Roll out the black and grey fondant to 3 mm thick and, using the building templates, cut enough buildings to circle the entire cake or create some designs of your own. Cut little rectangles from thinly rolled yellow fondant and glue into position as lights in the buildings. Rest the buildings on non-stick baking paper while you work. Position the buildings around the cake using tylose glue. Roll the remaining yellow fondant to a thickness of 3 mm and use a knife and the bat template to cut the bat light that shines in the sky. Glue this into position on the cake.

STAGE THREE

7. *Spider web.* Using the piping bag fitted with a number 2 tip and filled with black royal icing, pipe all the straight lines, starting at the cake and piping out to the edge of the board. Next add the curved webbing, starting with the row closest to the cake and working outwards.
8. *Stars.* Once the stars have set dry, position them on the cake by inserting the wires down into the cake at various depths.

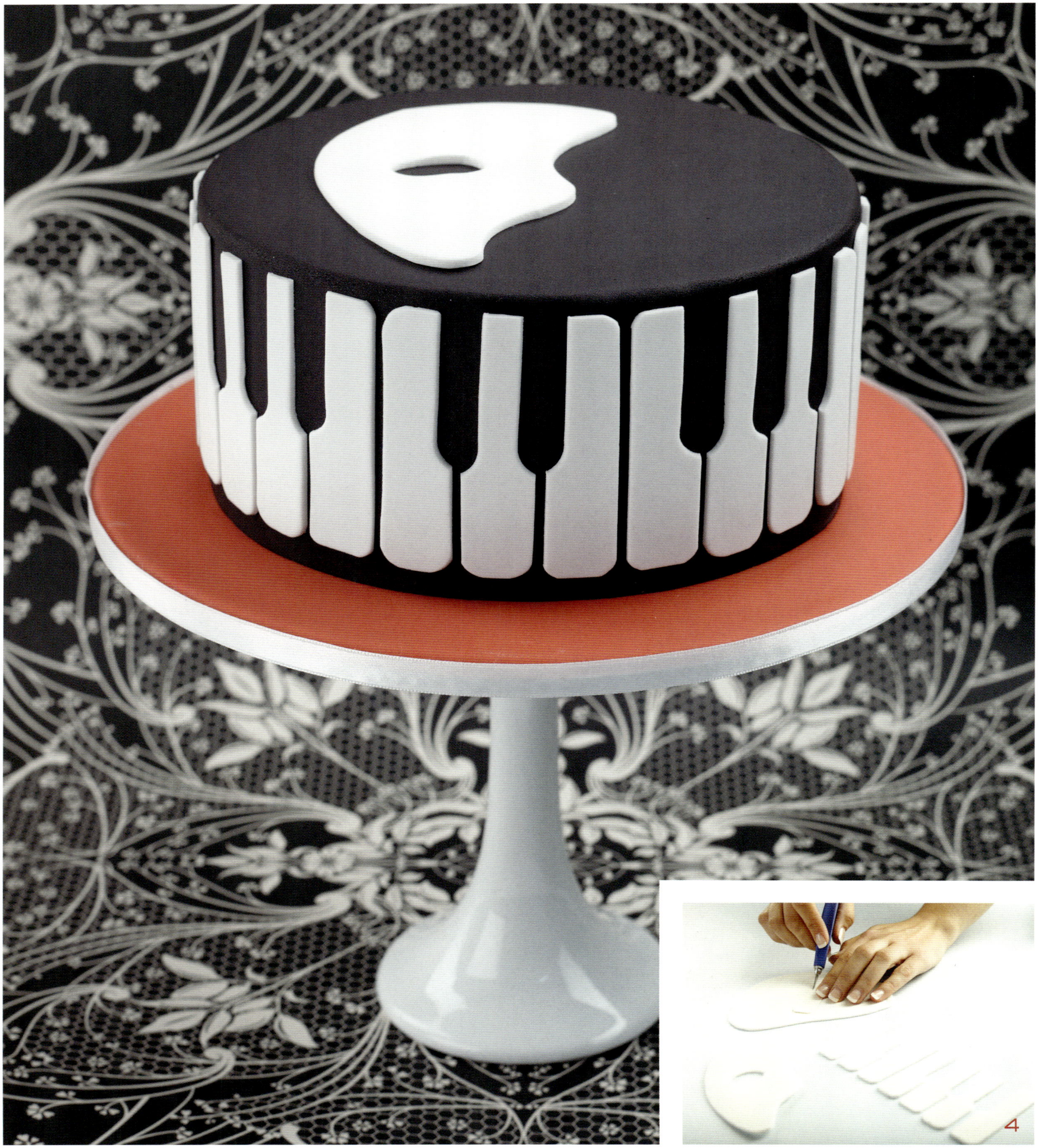
4

musical silhouette

Contrasting colours and simple shapes give this cake drama – perfect for budding musicians and music lovers.

CAKE REQUIREMENTS
- 1 x 18-cm (7") round cake (see pages 16–17)

DECORATING INGREDIENTS
- 1 x ganache recipe (see page 13)
- 1 x apricot glaze recipe (see page 15)
- 2 kg fondant icing (pre-coloured store-bought or coloured with gel paste food colouring), set aside in plastic wrap
    - 900 g black
    - 700 g red
    - 400 g white
- pure icing sugar (for kneading)
- cornflour (for rolling out)
- tylose glue (see page 15)
- tylose powder

EQUIPMENT
- 25-cm (10") round heavy cake board
- 1 m white ribbon (10–15 mm wide)
- templates (see page 138)
- serrated knife and palette knife
- scraper with straight edge
- pastry brush
- fine sieve (for sifting icing sugar when kneading)
- large and small rolling pins
- craft knife with fine pointed blade
- smoothers
- small paintbrush (for applying tylose glue)
- non-stick baking paper (for drying decorations)
- scissors and non-toxic glue

STAGE ONE
1. *Prepare cake.* Level cake, removing crust from top to give a flat surface, then invert so the trimmed surface becomes base of your cake. Secure cake to heavy board and cover with ganache (see page 19). Allow cake to set overnight, if possible.

STAGE TWO
2. *Cover cake.* Brush cake with apricot glaze and cover using kneaded black fondant. Smooth and trim off any excess fondant.
3. *Cover board.* Knead red fondant and roll out large enough to cover board. Cut an 18-cm (7") round from the centre, lift fondant over cake and onto board, fixing with tylose glue and smoothing and trimming. Trim with white ribbon and secure with non-toxic glue.
4. *Piano keys.* Knead tylose powder (see page 15) into 500 g of white fondant to make it firmer and easier to work with. Roll fondant out to a thickness of 3 mm and use a craft knife and the templates on page 138 to cut out 4 sets of piano keys and a single mask, placing the cut fondant pieces on a sheet of non-stick baking paper while you work. They will be easier to handle and keep their shape better if slightly set.
5. *Placing keys on cake.* Brush back of each key with tylose glue and place evenly spaced and in their correct order around cake. There is every chance your piano keys may not match up perfectly where you start and finish sticking them to the cake; make this the back of the cake where it is less noticeable.
6. *Mask.* Brush back with tylose glue and position on cake.

Use a fine-bladed craft knife to cut around templates. Wipe the blade clean regularly during the process to prevent sticking and messy edges.

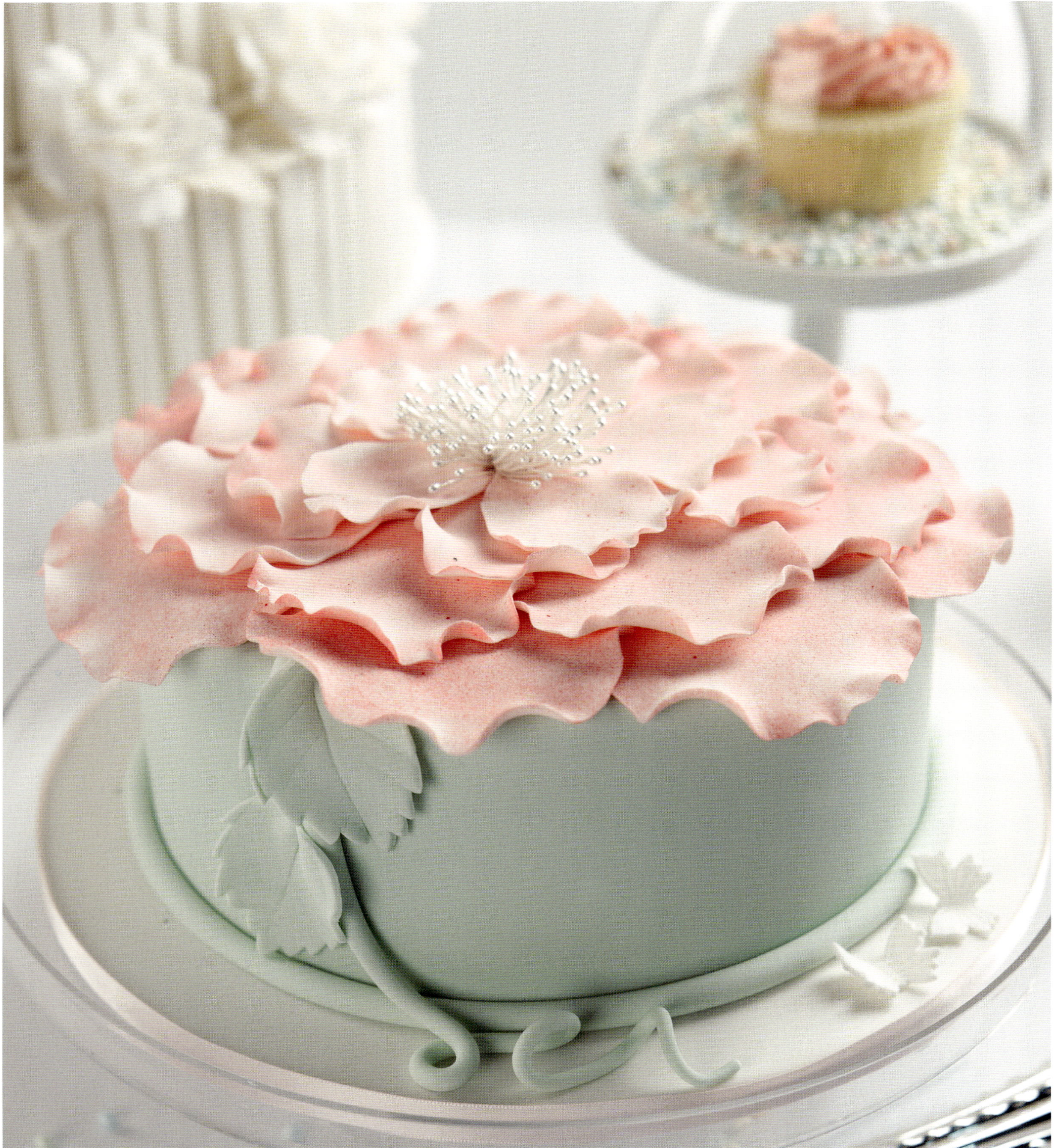

in full bloom

Many years ago, a customer brought in a party invitation that featured a beautiful open silk flower. I designed this simple cake for her and it has been a regular request ever since, often with a larger sugar butterfly delicately perched on a petal.

CAKE REQUIREMENTS

- 1 x 23-cm (9") round cake (see pages 16–17)

DECORATING INGREDIENTS

- 1 x ganache recipe (see page 13)
- 1 x royal icing recipe (see page 14)
- 1 x apricot glaze recipe (see page 15)
- 2.2 kg fondant icing (pre-coloured store-bought or coloured with gel paste food colouring), set aside in plastic wrap
    - 700 g white
    - 1.1 kg pale green
    - 400 g pale pink
- pure icing sugar (for kneading)
- cornflour (for rolling out and diluting powdered colouring)
- tylose powder
- tylose glue (see page 15)
- powdered pink food dust

EQUIPMENT

- 14-cm (11") round heavy cake board
- 1 m pale pink ribbon (10–15 mm wide)
- petal templates (see page 139)
- ½ length number 20 cake decorator's wire
- florist tape
- stamens
- serrated knife
- palette knife
- scraper with straight edge
- pastry brush
- fine sieve (for sifting icing sugar when kneading)
- large and small rolling pins
- knife
- smoothers
- large ball tool
- petal pad
- large leaf cutter
- Dresden tool or veining mat
- bowls (for drying petals)
- number 2 piping tip
- coupler and piping bag
- large soft paintbrush
- small paintbrush (for applying tylose glue)
- scissors
- non-toxic glue

A wide range of stamens (very thin wires with a bauble or pearl at the end) can be purchased from specialty cake decorating stores or online.

cakestar 38

STAGE ONE

1. *Prepare cake.* Level cake, removing crust from top to give a flat surface and invert so trimmed surface becomes base of your cake. Secure cake to heavy board and cover with ganache (see page 19). Allow cake to set overnight if, possible.
2. *Making petals.* Knead tylose powder (see page 15) into pale pink fondant. Working a petal at a time to avoid drying and cracking, roll out fondant to a thickness of 3 mm and use a knife and petal template to cut each petal. Immediately shape using a ball tool and flower mat to ruffle edges before drying them in bowls dusted with cornflour to avoid the petals sticking. You will need to make 7 large petals for the outer layer, 6 medium for the next layer, and 5 small for the centre layer. Allow petals to dry for several hours or overnight.

STAGE TWO

3. *Cover cake.* Brush cake with apricot glaze and cover using kneaded pale green fondant. Smooth and trim off any excess fondant.
4. *Cover board.* Knead white fondant and roll out a piece large enough to cover board. Cut a 23-cm (9") round from the centre, lift fondant over your cake and onto board, fixing with tylose glue and smoothing and trimming. Roll a snake of green fondant to cover the join between cake and iced board and glue in place with tylose glue. Trim board with pale pink ribbon, securing with non-toxic glue.

STAGE THREE

5. *Vines and leaves.* Knead tylose powder (see page 15) into the remaining pale green fondant. Roll a snake of icing, tapering one end using the smoother. Position this on the cake with the thicker end near the centre of the top of the cake and the tapered end trailing down the side and onto the iced cake board, creating natural-looking bends and loops. Use a leaf cutter to cut 2 leaves and mark veins with a veining mat or Dresden tool and attach these using tylose glue.
6. *Colour petals.* Mix powdered pink food dust with a little cornflour to lighten and use a large soft, dry paintbrush to add colour to the edges of each petal.
7. *Arrange petals.* Use royal icing to stick petals in position on cake, starting with larger petals on outer layer and working inwards.
8. *Centre.* Make a hook at the end of a piece of decorator's wire. Fold small bunches of stamens in half through the hook and secure with florist tape. Keep adding stamens in this way until you have a nice full bunch. Tape down the length of the wire and push into centre of cake.

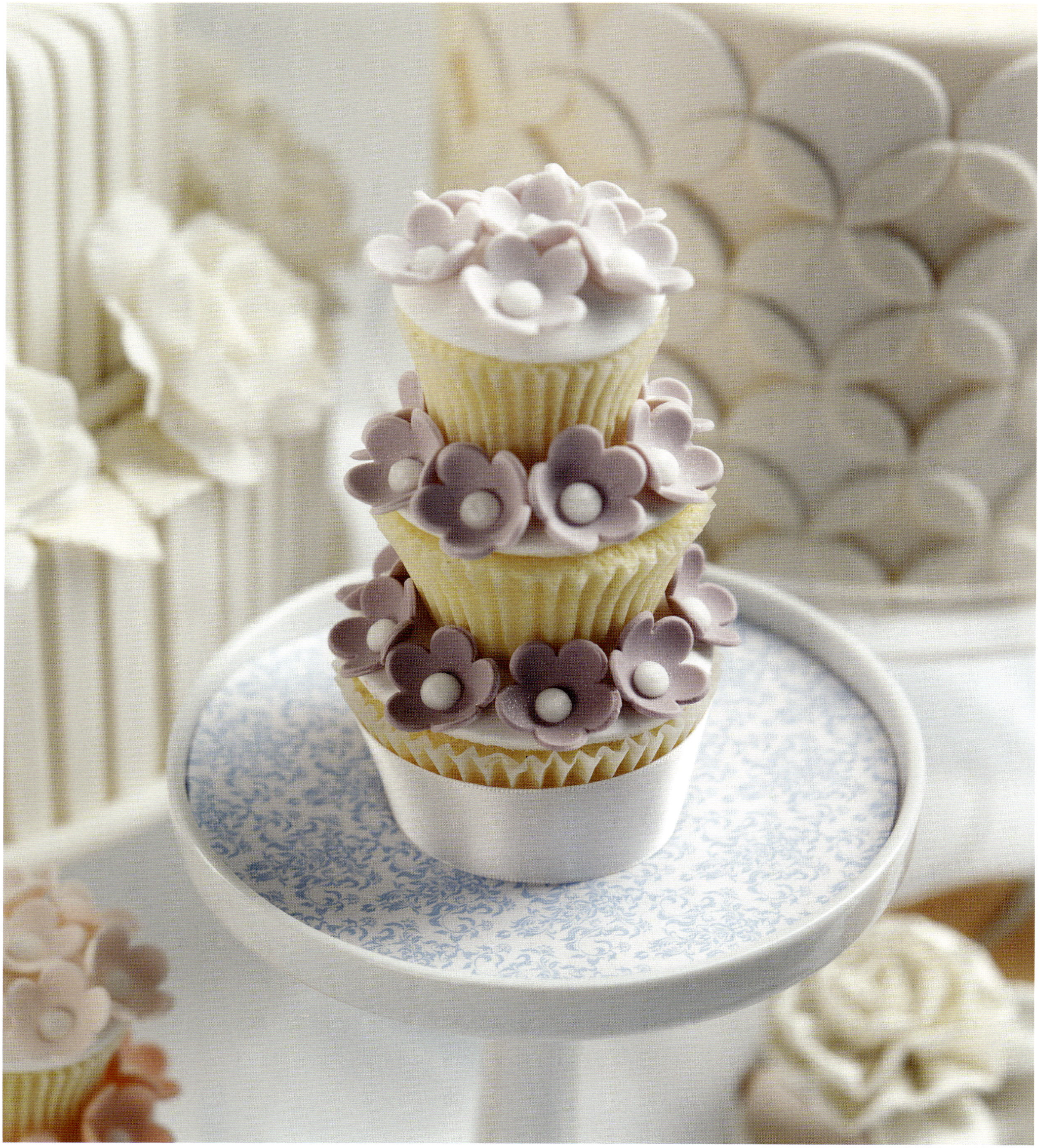

petit tiered cakes

I love displaying these tiny towers of cupcakes on candlestick holders for added height and drama. Imagine making a miniature wedding cake for each guest to take home. Makes 6.

CAKE REQUIREMENTS

- 6 mini cupcakes (see pages 16–17)
- 6 medium cupcakes (see pages 16–17)
- 6 large cupcakes (see pages 16–17)

DECORATING INGREDIENTS

- ½ x buttercream recipe (see recipe page 13)
- 1 x royal icing (see recipe page 14)
- 1.7 kg fondant icing (pre-coloured store-bought or coloured with gel paste food colouring), set aside in plastic wrap
    - 1.4 kg white
    - 100 g golden yellow
    - 100 g apricot
    - 100 g purple or blue
- pure icing sugar (for kneading)
- cornflour (for rolling out)
- tylose powder

EQUIPMENT

- small palette knife
- smoother
- number 2 piping tip
- coupler and piping bag
- 6 candy sticks
- fine sieve (for sifting icing sugar when kneading)
- small rolling pin
- circle cutters
- blossom cutter (2-cm diameter)
- petal pad
- ball tool
- small paintbrush (to tidy flower centres if necessary)
- scissors (to trim candy sticks if necessary)

Choose your own colour scheme to match the cupcake flowers with your party's theme. Even white flowers look elegant against the white fondant background.

cakestar 42

STAGE ONE

1. *Icing cupcakes.* Coat cupcakes in buttercream icing then fondant-ice in white (see page 21).
2. *Assembling.* Pipe a small amount of royal icing onto centre of each large cupcake. Place a medium cupcake on top of each, pipe a dot of royal icing onto the centre of each medium cupcake, then place a mini cupcake on top of each. Insert candy stick through centre of all three cakes to secure. If candy stick is too long for the height of your cupcakes, trim to level with the surface of top cupcake.

STAGE TWO

3. *Darkest flowers.* Knead tylose powder (see page 15) into each colour. On a work surface dusted with cornflour, roll out each colour to a very thin, even thickness and cut 9 flowers with blossom cutter to circle bottom layer of each cake (there is enough icing allowed to make up to 2 cakes of each colour). Shape blossoms by placing on a petal pad dusted with cornflour and press ball tool into centre of petal to make them cupped. Allow to dry.
4. *Medium flowers.* Add 50 g white fondant and another ½ teaspoon tylose powder to each colour to create a lighter version. Cut and shape 8 blossoms to circle the middle layer of each cake. Allow to dry.
5. *Lightest flowers.* Add a further 50 g of white fondant and another ½ teaspoon tylose powder to each colour to create a very, very pale shade. Cut and shape 7 blossoms to cover the top of each cake. Allow to dry.

STAGE THREE

6. *Arrange flowers.* Use small dots of royal icing to stick dried blossoms in place with bottom layer of each little cake tower being the darker flowers, lighter versions of the same colour for the second layer and the lightest for the top.
7. *Flower centres.* Pipe evenly sized dots of white royal icing in the centre of all blossoms and use a slightly dampened paintbrush to tidy peaks if needed.

Flowers for these little cakes can be made up to 2 weeks ahead, meaning less work on the day of the party. For an even quicker alternative you can use ready-made icing flowers (see edible decorations, page 11).

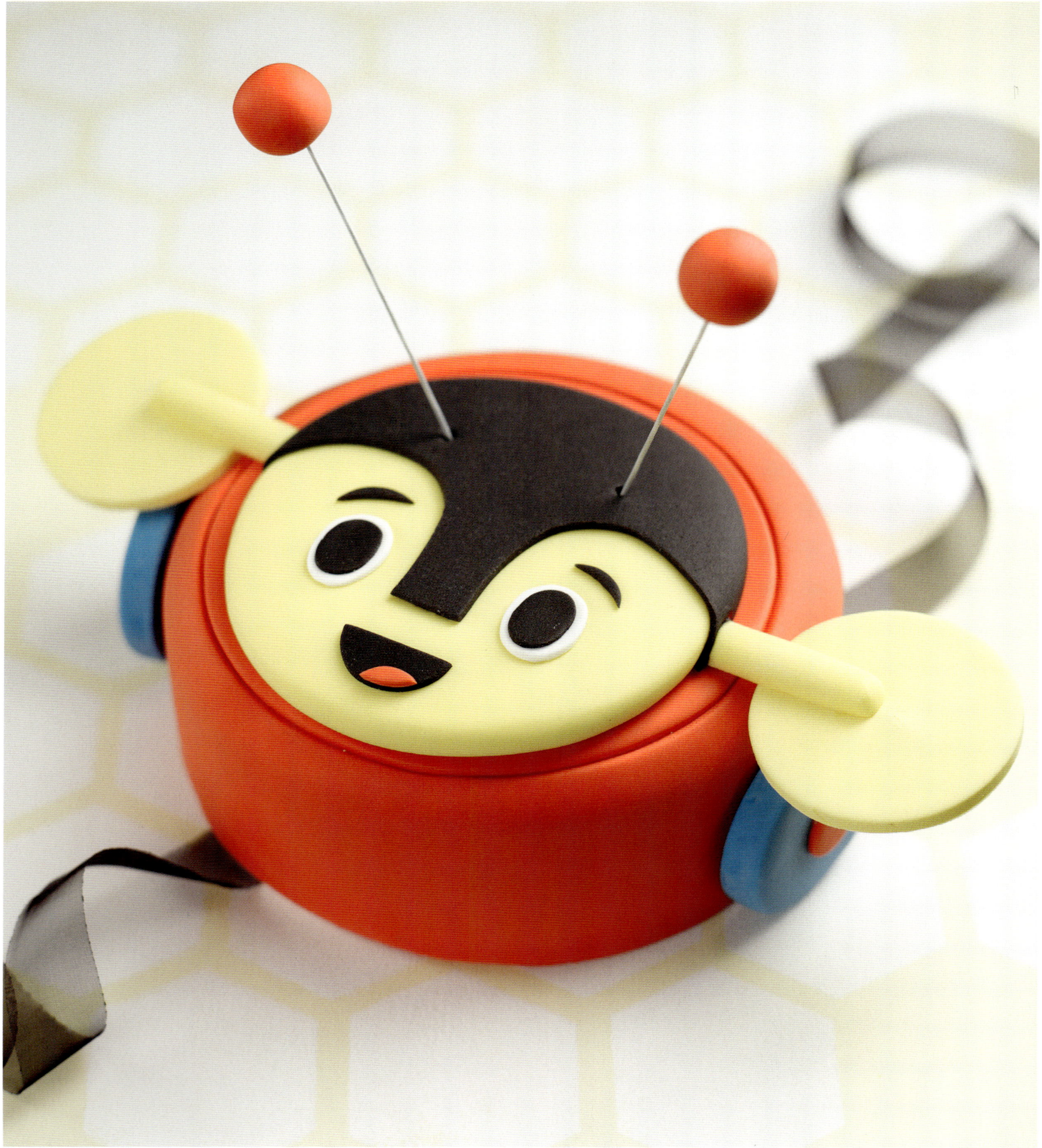

buzzing bee

A playful take on this iconic children's toy.

CAKE REQUIREMENTS
- 1 x 18-cm (7") round cake (see pages 16–17)

DECORATING INGREDIENTS
- 1 x ganache recipe (see page 13)
- 1 x apricot glaze recipe (see page 15)
- 1.7 kg fondant icing (pre-coloured store-bought or coloured with gel paste food colouring), set aside in plastic wrap
    - 500 g yellow
    - 100 g blue
    - 900 g red
    - 150 g black
    - 50 g white
- pure icing sugar (for kneading)
- cornflour (for rolling out)
- tylose powder
- tylose glue (see page 15)

EQUIPMENT
- 18-cm (7") round heavy cake board
- 15-cm (6") round cake board (to trace around)
- 2 cake decorator's wires (number 18)
- 2 wooden kitchen skewers
- face templates (see page 139)
- serrated knife
- large palette knife
- scraper with straight edge
- pastry brush
- fine sieve (for sifting icing sugar when kneading)
- large and small rolling pins
- knife
- circle cutters
- smoothers
- Dresden tool
- small paintbrush (for applying tylose glue)

cakestar 46

STAGE ONE

1. *Prepare cake.* Level cake, removing crust from top to give a flat surface, then invert so trimmed surface becomes the base of your cake. Secure cake to heavy board and cover with ganache (see page 19). Allow cake to set overnight, if possible.
2. *Wings.* Knead tylose powder (see page 15) into yellow fondant and roll out to a thickness of 5 mm. Use a 6-cm-diameter circle cutter to cut 2 rounds, inserting a kitchen skewer through each. Roll a snake of yellow fondant 5 cm long and 2 cm thick. Cut in half lengthwise and use tylose glue to stick each from the centre of each wing along the kitchen skewer. Rest on non-stick baking paper and allow to dry for several hours or overnight.
3. *Wheels.* Knead tylose powder (see page 15) into blue fondant, roll out to a thickness of 1 cm and cut 2 wheels using a 7-cm-diameter circle cutter. Roll out red fondant to 3 mm and cut 2 x 2.5-cm-diameter rounds, sticking onto the centre of the blue wheels using tylose glue. Rest on non-stick baking paper and allow to dry several hours or overnight.
4. *Antennae.* Knead tylose powder (see page 15) into 30 g of red fondant, divide in half and roll each into a ball. Wet the end of each decorator's wire before inserting one into each ball. Rest on non-stick baking paper and allow to dry overnight.

STAGE TWO

5. *Cover cake.* Brush cake with apricot glaze and cover with kneaded red fondant. Smooth and trim off any excess fondant.
6. *Indent cake.* While fondant is still soft, indent a 15-cm (6") diameter round by tracing around a cake board with a Dresden tool.
7. *Face.* Roll the remaining yellow fondant into a ball and flatten into a 12.5-cm (5") diameter disc using your hands and a small rolling pin. Use the templates on page 139 to cut the nose piece from black fondant kneaded and rolled out to a thickness of 3 mm. Use tylose glue to stick in place, smoothing over the curved edge of the disk. The mouth is half of a 3-cm round of thinly rolled black fondant with a small piece of red fondant overlayed and trimmed to size.
8. *Eyes.* Roll out the black and white fondant to a thickness of 3 mm. Cut 2 white rounds using a 2-cm-diameter cutter and lengthen into an oval shape by rolling with a rolling pin. Cut 2 black rounds using a 1.5-cm-diameter cutter, and lengthen using same technique. Use tylose glue to stick the black pupils on top of the white eyes and attach to the face.
9. *Eyebrows.* Roll out the black fondant to a thickness of 3 mm, cut out a 2-cm-diameter round and cut 2 eyebrows from this using a knife. Stick in place using tylose glue.

STAGE THREE

10. *Assembly.* Place the completed face on top of the cake, gluing into position with tylose glue. Insert the antennae. Insert the skewers from the wings into the cake just underneath the face. Glue the wheels in position on the side.

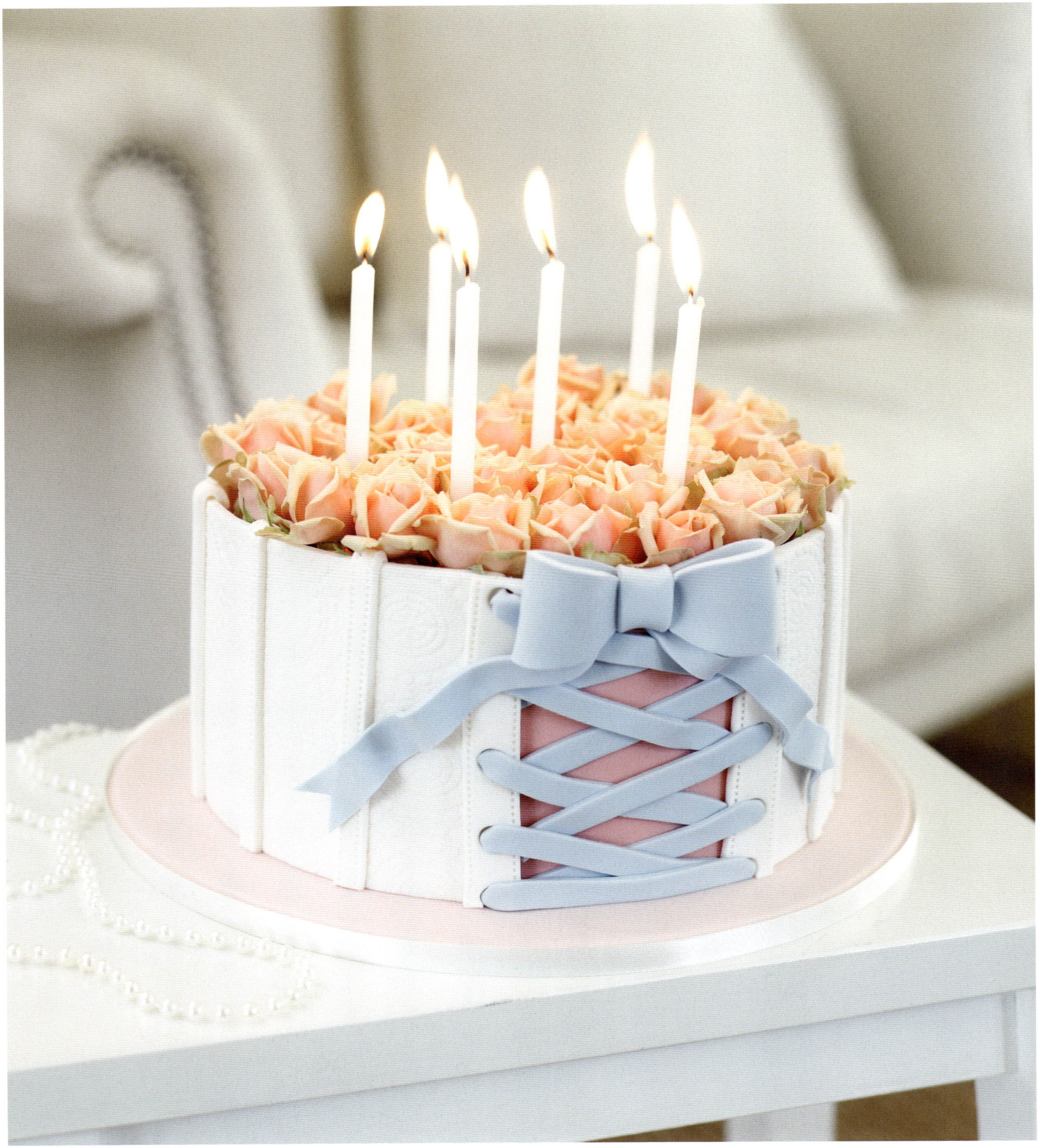

laced up

The fashion world is always a great place to find ideas for cakes. This corset-inspired design is delicate and feminine in soft colours or a little more racy in red and black. Alter the colours or replace the fresh roses with chocolates.

CAKE REQUIREMENTS

- 1 x 20-cm (8") round cake (see pages 16–17)

DECORATING INGREDIENTS

- 1 x ganache recipe (see page 13)
- 1 x apricot glaze recipe (see page 15)
- 2.5 kg fondant icing (pre-coloured store-bought or coloured with gel paste food colouring), set aside in plastic wrap
    - 800 g medium pink
    - 700 g pale pink
    - 800 g ivory
    - 200 g pale blue
- pure icing sugar (for kneading)
- cornflour (for rolling out)
- tylose powder
- tylose glue (see page 15)
- fresh roses

EQUIPMENT

- 28-cm (11") round heavy board
- 1 m white ribbon (10 mm wide)
- serrated knife
- large palette knife
- scraper with straight edge
- pastry brush
- fine sieve (for sifting icing sugar when kneading)
- large and small rolling pins
- knife
- smoothers
- piece of lace or fabric with raised pattern
- measuring tape
- ruler
- stitching tool
- pound piping tip (to cut holes for laces)
- small paintbrush (for applying tylose glue)
- scissors
- bow template (see page 138)
- non-toxic craft glue
- florist tape

cakestar 50

STAGE ONE

1. *Prepare cake.* Level cake, removing crust from top to give a flat surface. Invert so trimmed surface becomes the base of your cake. Secure cake to heavy board and cover with ganache (see page 19). Allow cake to set overnight, if possible.

STAGE TWO

2. *Cover cake.* Brush cake with apricot glaze and cover with kneaded medium pink fondant. Smooth and trim off any excess fondant.
3. *Cover board.* Knead pale pink fondant and roll out to a piece large enough to cover board. Cut a 20-cm (8") round from the centre and lift fondant over cake and onto board, fixing with tylose glue and smoothing and trimming. Trim edge of the board with ribbon, using non-toxic glue to fasten.
4. *Embossing corset.* Knead tylose (see page 15) into ivory fondant to make it more manageable when creating the wrapped corset effect. Measure height of your iced cake. On a surface dusted with cornflour, roll out ivory fondant to a length of 65 cm and width equal to height of your cake plus an extra 1 cm. Working quickly to ensure icing does not dry and crack, place lace or patterned fabric on fondant and gently apply pressure with your rolling pin to leave an embossed pattern. Lift off lace and use knife and ruler to trim exactly to size.
5. *Applying embossed icing to cake.* Brush sides of cake with tylose glue, leaving a section unglued where laced opening will be at the front of the cake. Roll up ivory fondant with pattern facing the inside of the roll, then unroll into position around cake.
6. *Stitched panels.* Cut 2 strips of ivory fondant icing 1.5 cm wide and a little longer than the height of corset. Mark both edges with stitching tool and cut holes for laces using a large round piping tip. Use tylose glue to fix to ends of corset panel.
7. Cut 11 thinner strips of the same length, mark with stitching tool and glue in place with even spacing around corset pane.

STAGE THREE

8. *Laced panel.* Add tylose to pale blue fondant icing. Roll out thinly and cut strips 7.5 mm wide. Form these into a crisscross pattern over open panel, placing a final strip across base of panel and attaching with tylose glue.
9. *Bow.* Roll out remaining blue fondant thinly and use template on page 138 as a guide to cut out the 5 pieces forming the bow. The tail pieces of the bow are attached to the cake first with tylose glue. Create bow by folding long edges of bow piece into the centre and attaching with tylose glue. The small centre or knot piece is then glued in place. Attach bow to cake over tail pieces using tylose glue. (If the weight of the bow is pulling it off the cake, support it using 2 carefully placed cocktail sticks until fondant and glue dry.)

STAGE FOUR

10. *Finishing touches.* Trim heads from roses, leaving 2 cm of stem. Wrap stems with florist tape to avoid contact with cake and place these in position to fill surface of the cake.

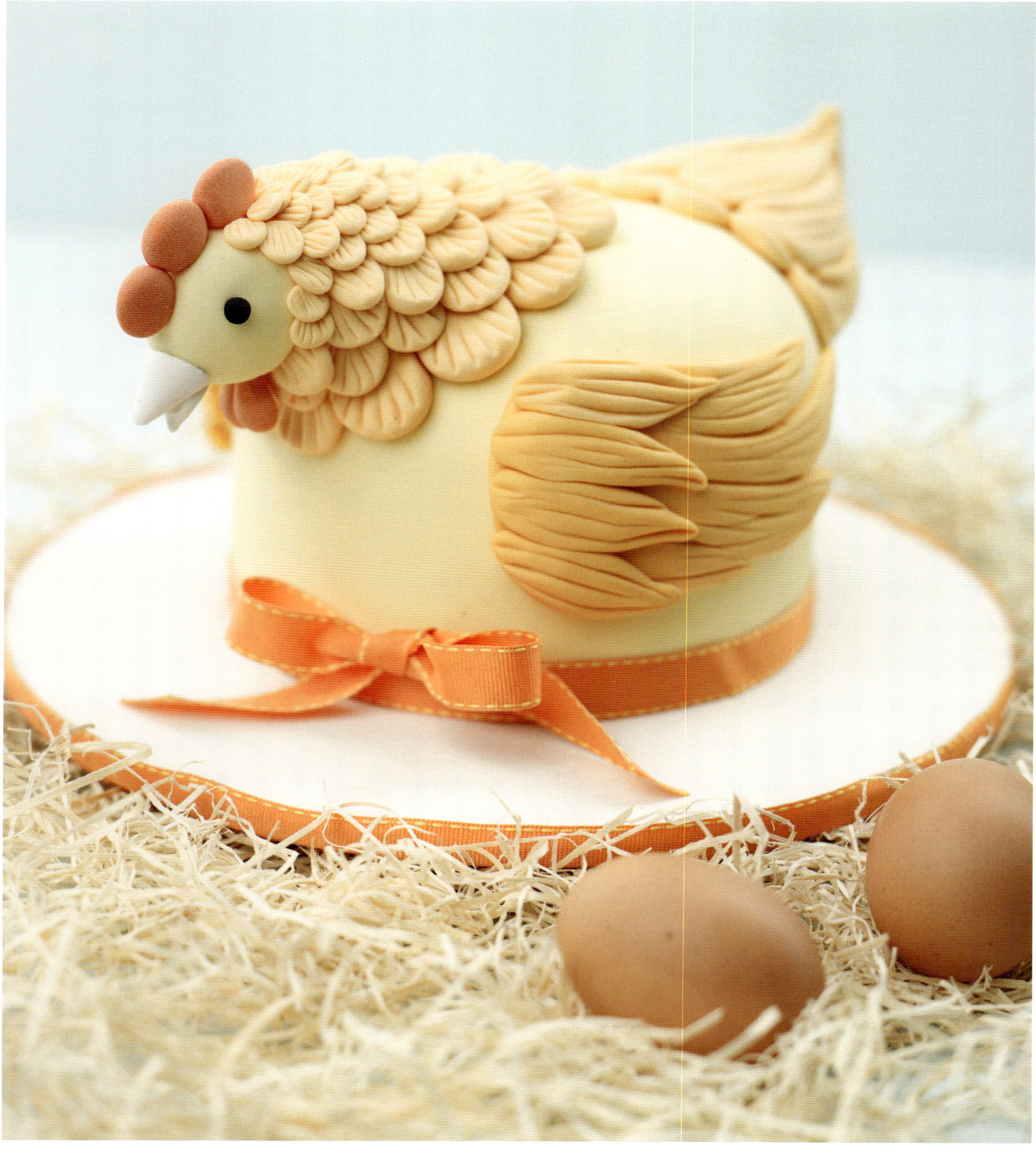

so chic

Perfect for a cute chick, hen-pecked husband, hen's day, Mother Hen or even a farmyard party, this cake is surprisingly simple to make and would look beautiful in any colour combination. At CakeStar we make a glammed-up white and pink hen fitted with a tulle veil as a centrepiece for a hen's afternoon tea.

CAKE REQUIREMENTS

- 1 x 15-cm (6") round cake (see pages 16–17)
- ½ x 15-cm ball cake (see pages 16–17)

DECORATING INGREDIENTS

- 1 x ganache recipe (see page 13)
- 1 x apricot glaze recipe (see page 15)
- 2.54 kg fondant icing (pre-coloured store-bought, or coloured with gel paste food colouring), set aside in plastic wrap
    - 1 kg pale yellow
    - 700 g white
    - 800 g pale orange
    - 35 g deep orange
    - 5 g black
- pure icing sugar (for kneading)
- cornflour (for rolling out)
- tylose powder
- tylose glue (see page 15)

EQUIPMENT

- 28-cm (11") round heavy cake board
- 1.6 m orange ribbon (10–15 mm wide)
- serrated knife
- large palette knife
- scraper with straight edge
- strip of cardboard from a milk carton (for smoothing curved ganache surface)
- pastry brush
- fine sieve (for sifting icing sugar when kneading)
- large rolling pin
- knife
- smoothers
- Dresden tool
- small paintbrush (for applying tylose glue)
- 2 wooden kitchen skewers
- non-toxic craft glue
- scissors
- wing template (see page 136)

cakestar 54

STAGE ONE

1. *Prepare cakes.* Level both cakes, removing crust from top to give a flat surface, then fix ball cake on top of round cake using ganache. Use a serrated knife to sculpt or correct the shape wherever necessary. Secure cake to heavy board and cover with ganache (see page 19). Allow cake to set overnight, if possible.

STAGE TWO

2. *Cover cake.* Brush cake with apricot glaze and cover in kneaded pale yellow fondant. Smooth and trim off any excess fondant.
3. *Cover board.* Knead white fondant and roll out to a piece large enough to cover board. Cut a 15-cm (6") round from the centre, lift fondant over cake and onto board, fixing with tylose glue, smoothing and trimming as per the instructions on page 21. Trim edge of board with orange ribbon, using non-toxic glue to fasten.
4. *Building up shape.* The head and tail sections will need to be strengthened with tylose powder, which will allow them to set in shape. Knead tylose powder (see page 15) into remaining pale yellow fondant, then take 200 g of this to form into a conical shape, bending the head into desired position and flattening slightly so head is more narrow than base of the neck. Form another 200 g into a cone shape – this will become the foundation for the hen's tail. Attach these to the cake using tylose glue, and insert a kitchen skewer through each and into the cake as support. The features will conceal the kitchen skewer.

STAGE THREE

5. *Feathers.* To create feathered effect on the neck and head, you will need to make four different-sized feathers, with larger feathers being placed at the base of the neck, working up to smaller feathers near the hen's face. To ensure feathers in each row are fairly uniform in size, begin by rolling a sausage of the pale orange icing to the thickness of your thumb, then cut this into around 16 equal-sized portions. Roll each into a ball, flattening and marking with a Dresden tool or knife. For next rows of feathers, roll sausages slightly thinner and cut to make smaller feathers. Attach feathers with tylose glue.
6. *Tail.* The tail is created by first covering the join at the base with medium-sized rounded feathers as made for the hen's neck. The rest is quickly assembled by rolling long teardrop-shaped pieces of fondant, which are flattened, indented with the Dresden tool and attached with tylose glue.
7. *Wings.* To make the wings, roll the remaining pale orange fondant out to a thickness of around 5 mm and cut mirror-image wing shapes using the wing template. Indent with some feathering, then use any offcuts to overlay a shorter row of feathers on each wing for texture. Stick wings in place.

STAGE FOUR

8. *Comb.* Knead a pinch of tylose powder into deep orange fondant. Divide this into 4 equal parts. Roll 3 into balls and flatten balls to make hen's comb. Attach in a row using tylose glue.
9. *Finishing touches.* Use remaining deep orange fondant to make hen's cheek flaps. Roll into a sausage, making it thinner in the centre and thicker at each end. Fold in half and attach fold underneath the hen's chin using tylose glue. To make beak, roll a small cone of white fondant and attach. The eyes are 2 tiny, equal-sized balls of black fondant. I love to tie a big bow around the base of the chicken.

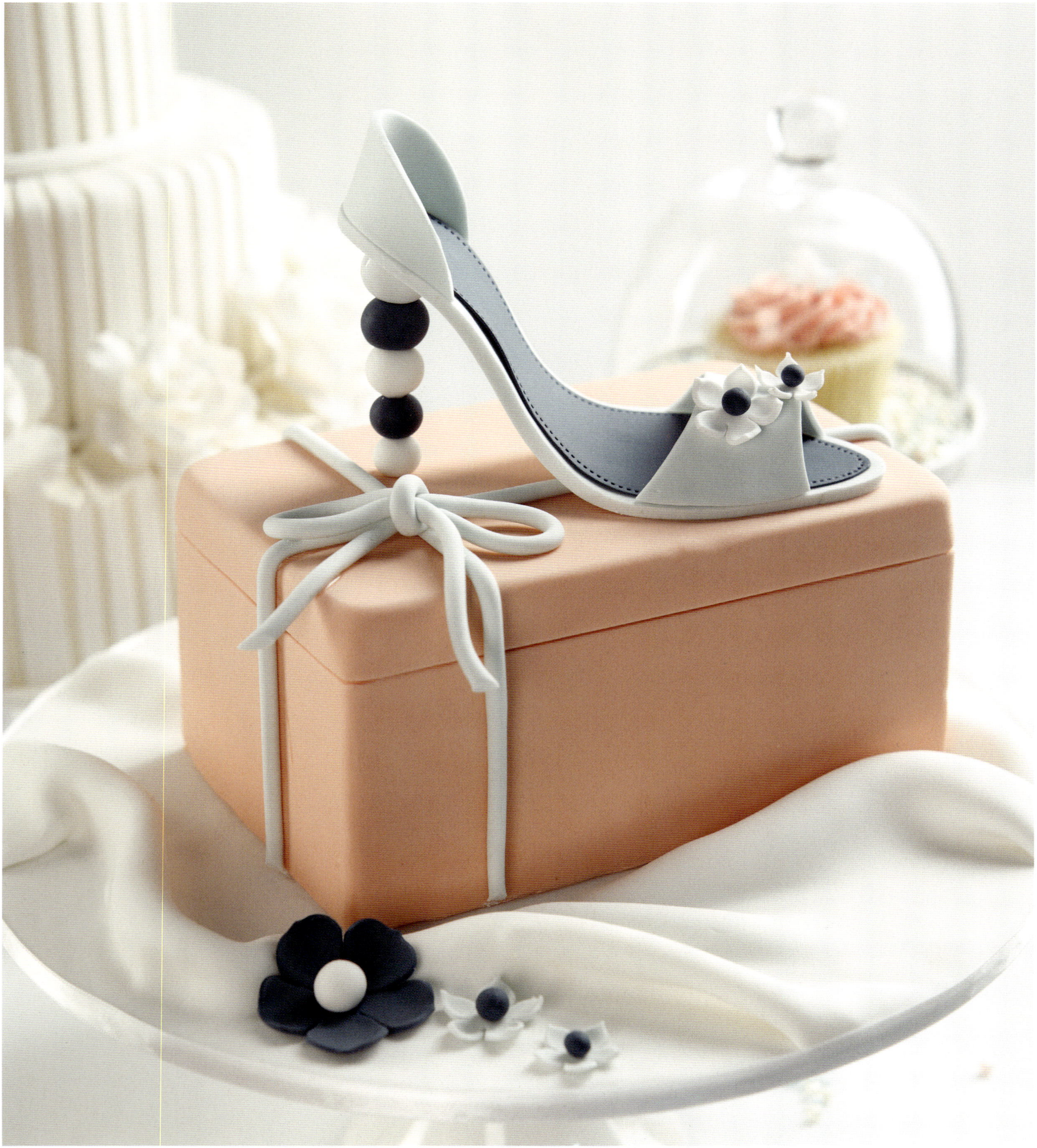

perfect fit

These shoes will satisfy both the tastebuds and the Imelda in us all.

CAKE REQUIREMENTS
- 1 x 20-cm (8") square cake (see pages 16–17)

DECORATING INGREDIENTS
- 1 x ganache recipe (see page 13)
- 1 x apricot glaze recipe (see page 15)
- ½ x royal icing recipe (see page 14)
- 2.3 kg fondant icing (pre-coloured store-bought or coloured with gel paste food colouring), set aside in plastic wrap
    - 200 g pale blue
    - 100 g navy blue
    - 1.2 kg peach
    - 800 g white
- pure icing sugar (for kneading)
- cornflour (for rolling out)
- tylose powder
- tylose glue (see page 15)

EQUIPMENT
- 33-cm (13") round heavy cake board
- 1 m white ribbon (10–15 mm wide)
- 1 thin wooden kitchen skewer
- templates (see page 141)
- non-stick baking paper
- serrated knife
- large palette knife
- scraper with straight edge
- pastry brush
- fine sieve (for sifting icing sugar when kneading)
- large and small rolling pins
- knife
- craft knife
- smoothers
- small paintbrush (for applying tylose glue)
- number 2 piping tip
- coupler and piping bag
- non-stick baking paper (for drying decorations)
- cup (for drying sole of shoe)
- stitching tool
- flower cutters
- petal pad
- small ball tool
- ruler
- scissors
- non-toxic glue

To allow maximum drying time, the shoe must be made at least 2 days before the cake is decorated.

cakestar 58

STAGE ONE

1. *Shoe sole.* Knead tylose powder (see page 15) into pale blue fondant and roll out to 5 mm thick. Use knife or craft knife to cut around sole template. Sit a small cup on a sheet of non-stick baking paper and drape icing over this to dry in shape.
2. *Shoe lining.* Knead tylose powder (see page 15) into navy blue fondant, roll out to a thickness of 3 mm and cut lining for shoe using template on page 141. Use stitching tool to mark a stitched outline before gluing lining to sole with tylose glue.
3. *Shoe toe and back.* Roll out pale blue fondant to 5 mm thick and use templates and knife to cut pieces for toe and back of shoe. Bend into position and glue with tylose glue.
4. *Heel.* Measure height of cup supporting shoe sole as it dries; this is how high the heel will have to be. Knead tylose powder (see page 15) into white fondant. Roll small balls of navy blue and white fondant and thread together on a skewer dampened with tylose glue, alternating colours. Trim skewer level with top ball, but leave pointed end protruding at the bottom, as this will later be pushed into the cake to stabilise the shoe.
5. Allow all parts of shoe to dry for at least 48 hours before removing from drying supports.

STAGE TWO

6. *Prepare cake.* Level cake, removing crust from top. Use serrated knife to cut in half and sandwich one half on top of the other using ganache (see page 19). Trim with serrated knife to correct shape wherever necessary. Lift cake onto a sheet of non-stick baking paper and cover with ganache (see page 19). Allow cake to set overnight, if possible.

STAGE THREE

7. *Cover cake.* Brush cake with apricot glaze and cover using kneaded peach fondant. Smooth and trim off any excess fondant.
8. *Mark lid.* While fondant on cake is still soft, use ruler to indent a line 2 cm from top of cake on all four sides. This will give the appearance of a shoebox and lid. If the cake moves while working, hold it in place using a smoother.
9. *Cover board.* Brush board with tylose glue. Knead white fondant and roll out a little larger than the board. Arrange fondant on board, leaving drapes and folds for fabric-like texture. Smooth and trim edges of fondant. Trim edge of cake board with ribbon, using non-toxic glue to fasten.
10. *Position cake.* While fondant on cake board is still soft, pipe a large dot of royal icing in the centre of the board. Carefully remove cake from baking paper and lift it into position, pressing down with a smoother to secure.

STAGE FOUR

11. *Assemble shoe.* Determine where on the shoebox you would like your shoe to sit and press the skewer that extends from the bottom of the heel into the cake. Use a small dot of royal icing underneath to secure. Put a dot of royal icing on the top of the heel and under the toe of the shoe. Carefully position shoe on heel and shoebox, wipe away any untidy royal icing with a damp paintbrush and allow royal icing to set a little.
12. *Decorating shoe.* The shoe can be decorated while it is drying or at the end of the project. On a surface dusted with cornflour, roll out white, pale blue and navy blue fondant to a very thin, even thickness and cut 1 or 2 flowers of each colour using various cutters. Give blossoms shape by placing on a petal pad dusted with cornflour and press ball tool into centre to make them cupped. The centres are tiny rolled balls of fondant. Glue flowers and centres in position on shoe and cake board.
13. *Twine on box.* The twine on the box is made by rolling 2 long thin snakes of pale blue fondant and gluing in place, trimming ends of each at base of cake. The bow is made up of 5 separate snakes of icing: 2 for tails, 2 bent to form loops of bow and a short cross piece for knot. Tails are glued in place first, followed by loops and then crosspiece covers joins.

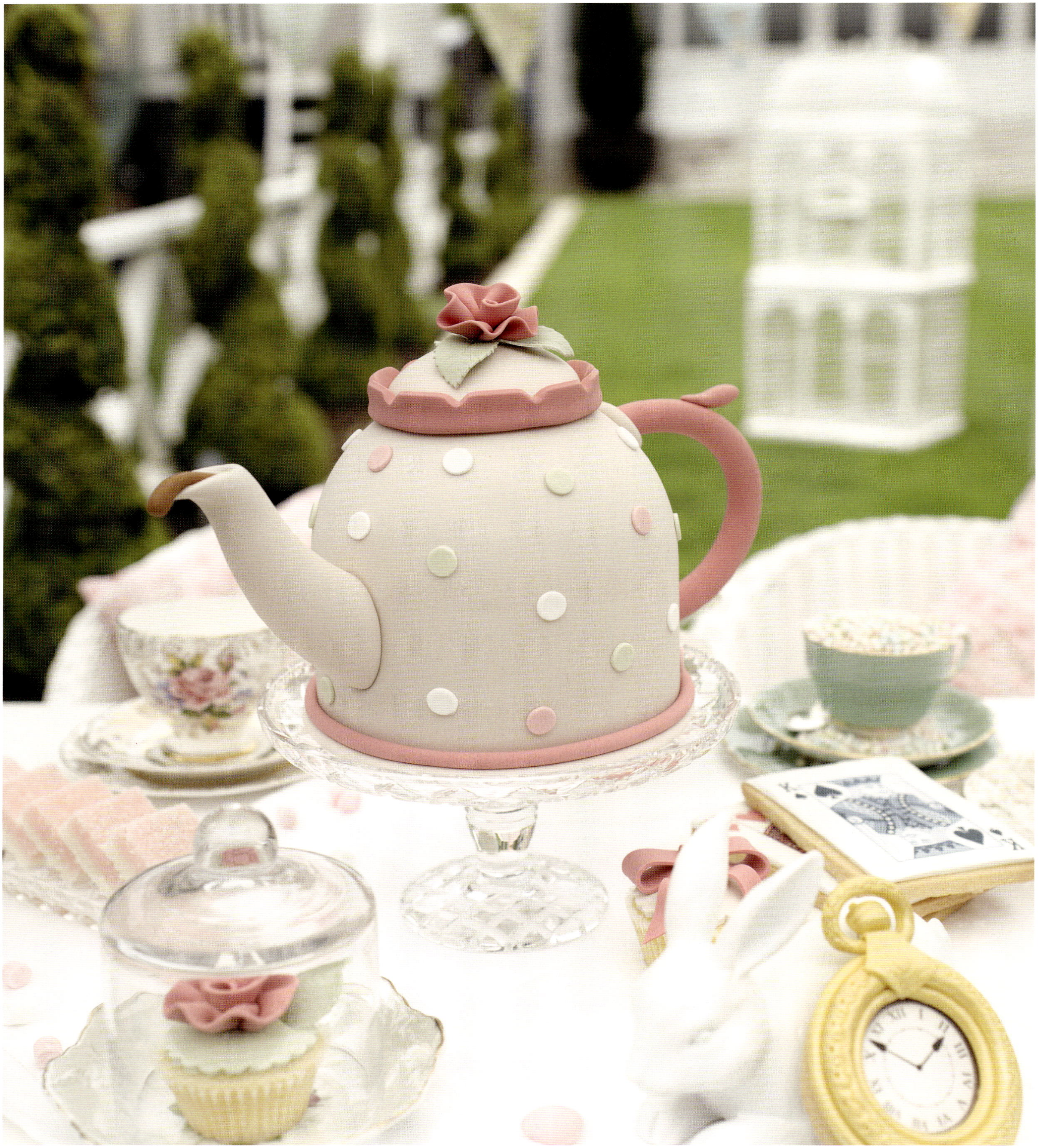

teatale party

Brew the perfect pot of tea for a tea party straight from the pages of a fairytale book. I have made hundreds of variations of this cake for occasions from baby showers to 100th birthdays.

CAKE REQUIREMENTS

- 1 x 15-cm (6") round cake (see pages 16–17)
- 1 x 15-cm (6") ball cake (see pages 16–17)

DECORATING INGREDIENTS

- 1 x ganache recipe (see page 13)
- 1 x apricot glaze recipe (see page 15)
- 2.31 kg fondant icing (pre-coloured store-bought or coloured with gel paste food colouring), set aside in plastic wrap
    - 1.2 kg pale pink (I like to add a touch of brown)
    - 700 g pale green
    - 350 g medium pink
    - 10 g brown
    - 50 g white
- pure icing sugar (for kneading)
- cornflour (for rolling out)
- tylose powder
- tylose glue (see page 15)

EQUIPMENT

- 25-cm (10") round heavy cake board
- 1 m white ribbon (10–15 mm wide)
- cake decorator's wire (number 18)
- 1 wooden kitchen skewer
- serrated knife
- large palette knife
- scraper with straight edge
- strip of cardboard from a milk carton (for smoothing curved ganache surface)
- pastry brush
- fine sieve (for sifting icing sugar when kneading)
- large and small rolling pins
- knife
- smoothers
- leaf cutter
- leaf veiner
- small paintbrush (for applying tylose powder)
- ruler and measuring tape
- non-stick baking paper (for drying decorations)
- scissors
- non-toxic glue

3

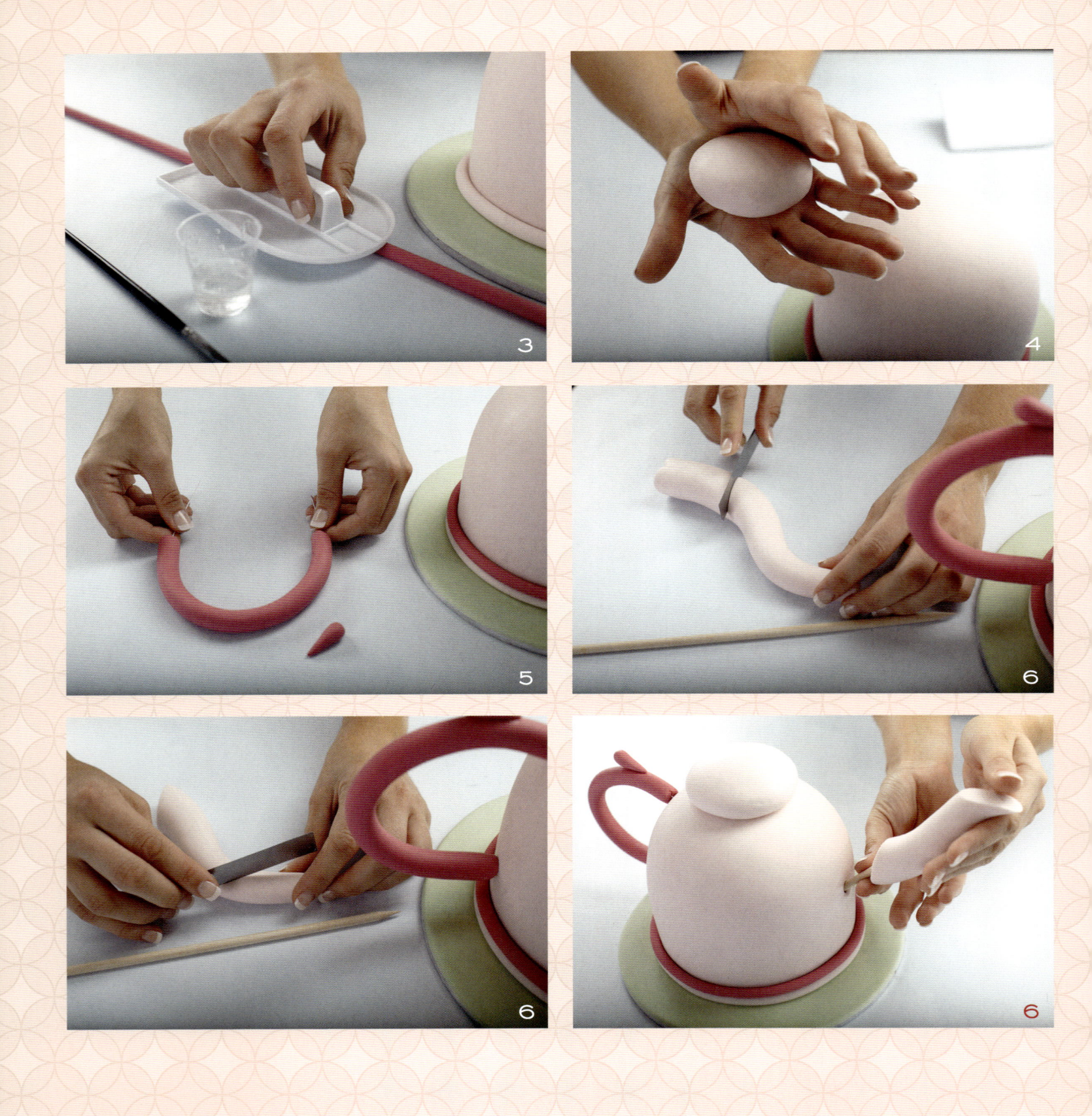

4

5

6

6

6

STAGE ONE

1. *Prepare cakes.* Level both cakes, removing crust from top to give a flat surface, then fix ball cake on top of round cake using ganache. Use a serrated knife to sculpt or correct shape wherever necessary. Secure cake to heavy board and cover with ganache (see page 19). Allow cake to set overnight, if possible.

STAGE TWO

2. *Cover cake.* Brush cake with apricot glaze and cover with kneaded soft pink fondant. Smooth and trim off any excess fondant.
3. *Cover board.* Knead green fondant and roll out large enough to cover board. Cut a 15-cm (6") round from the centre, lift over cake and onto board, fixing with tylose glue and smoothing and trimming. Roll a snake of soft pink icing and glue with tylose glue around the base of the cake to conceal join between cake and board. Repeat with medium pink to form a second band. Trim edge of cake board with ribbon, securing with non-toxic glue.
4. *Lid.* Knead tylose powder (see page 15) into remaining soft pink fondant. Roll 150 g into a ball then flatten to give a base using your hands. Use tylose glue to attach to the centre of the top of your cake.
5. *Handle.* Knead tylose powder (see page 15) into remaining medium pink fondant. Roll a snake of icing around 2 cm thick and 20 cm long. Brush full length of a cake decorating wire with tylose glue and insert into fondant from one end through to the other, allowing each end of the wire to protrude equally. Hold each end of the wire and bend fondant into handle shape. Roll a small teardrop of medium pink fondant. Position handle on the cake by inserting wires into the cake and gluing the joins with tylose glue. Add teardrop detail once the handle is in place.
6. *Spout.* Roll soft pink fondant (containing tylose powder) into a 4-cm thick sausage shape, narrowing what will be the spout end. Bend into desired position, trim thicker end flat to fit against the teapot and thinner end at an angle of 45 degrees to form spout. Insert wooden kitchen skewer through from the thick end, leaving a few centimetres of skewer showing that will go into the cake for support. Position spout on teapot, adhering with tylose glue. Should spout pull away from cake before it is set, prop up with clean, dry foam sponges until sufficiently dried.

STAGE THREE

7. *Rose handle.* Very thinly roll out medium pink fondant into a strip 6 cm wide and 20 cm long. Fold the strip in half lengthwise and use the paintbrush to run a line of tylose glue along the bottom edge (where the edges meet). Begin rolling up the strip, tightly at first for the inner layers of the rose then more loosely and with added ruffles formed by pinching together the icing at the base as you get to the outer, fuller layers. Pinch together your completed rose at the base and trim with scissors to neaten, if necessary. Thinly roll soft green fondant, cut 3 leaves using the leaf cutter, dust the surface of each with a tiny amount of cornflour then indent with the leaf veiner. If you do not have a veiner, you can use a Dresden tool or knife. Glue the leaves in place with tylose glue on the top of the teapot and then fix the rose.

8. *Lid detail.* Roll a 2-cm-thick snake of icing long enough to reach around outside of the teapot lid. Use the heel of your hand to thin one edge slightly then make regular indents along this thinner edge to give a scalloped pattern. Glue in place around the teapot lid with tylose glue.

9. *Spots.* Roll out remaining white, green and medium pink fondant to 3 mm thick. Use a large round piping tip or small circle cutter to cut out spots for your teapot. Arrange so they are evenly distributed over the teapot, gluing in place with tylose glue.

10. *Drop of tea.* Roll a 1-cm-diameter ball of brown fondant, working one side between your hands to form this into a teardrop shape. Glue in place on the spout of the teapot.

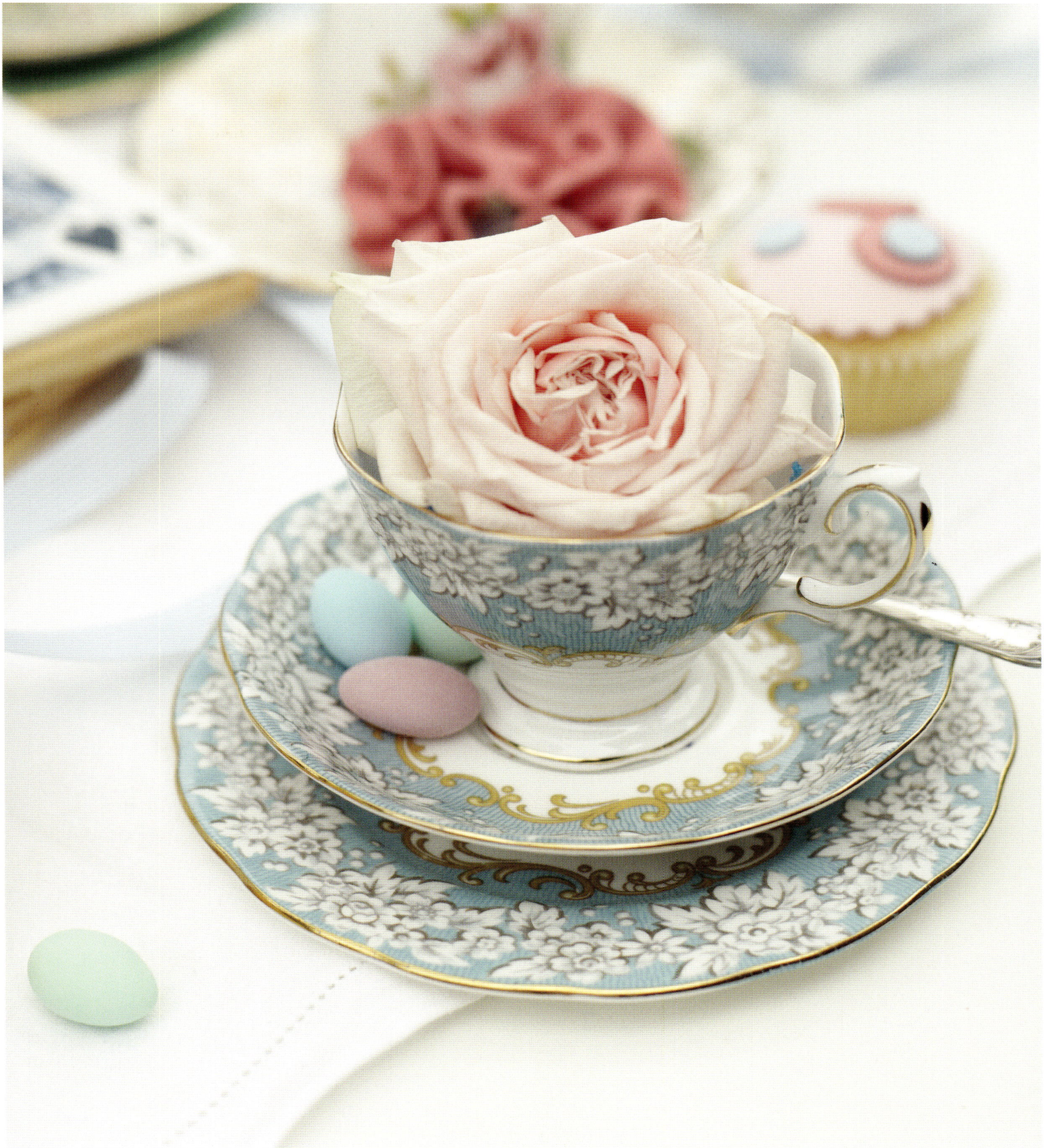

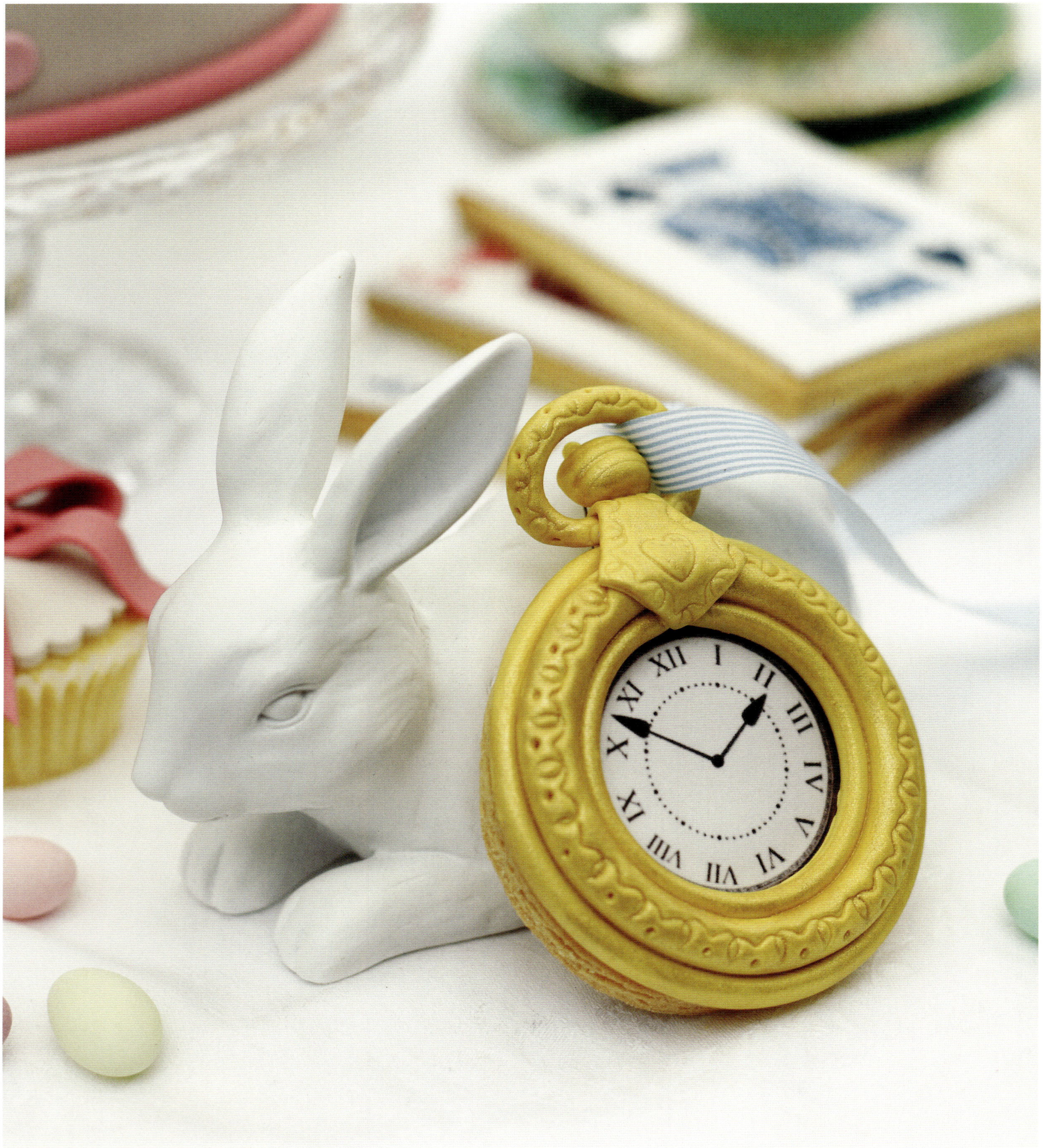

a wonderful time

Delectable timepieces set a whimsical scene for a mad hatter's tea party. Makes 12 biscuits.

CAKE REQUIREMENTS
- 12 x 8-cm diameter round biscuits (see page 18)

DECORATING INGREDIENTS
- 1 x royal icing recipe (see page 14)
- 1.56 kg fondant icing (pre-coloured store-bought or coloured with gel paste food colouring), set aside in plastic wrap
    - 600 g white
    - 960 g golden yellow
- pure icing sugar (for kneading)
- cornflour (for rolling out)
- tylose powder
- tylose glue (see page 15)
- edible images of clock faces of 5-cm diameter
- edible gold lustre
- decorator's alcohol or vodka

EQUIPMENT
- fine sieve (for sifting icing sugar when kneading)
- small rolling pin
- smoother
- circle cutters
- 1.5-cm heart cutter
- knife
- small paintbrush (for applying tylose glue)
- cocktail sticks
- number 2 piping tip
- coupler and piping bag

You can order custom-made edible images online, or just draw your own numerals on with a food-colouring pen.

cakestar 68

STAGE ONE

1. *Icing biscuits.* With same cutter used to cut biscuit shapes, cut rounds from white fondant rolled out to 3 mm thick. Stick in place using royal icing and smooth (see page 22).

STAGE TWO

2. *Clock faces.* Use 5-cm circle cutter to cut around each clock face. Carefully remove from backing sheet and glue in place in centre of iced biscuits using a small amount of tylose glue.
3. *Border.* Working with one biscuit at a time so the icing doesn't dry and crack, roll 2 thin and 1 medium-thickness snakes of golden yellow icing, each around 30 cm long. Make indents along thicker piece using edge of heart cutter, overlapping each slightly to give pattern, and add more detail with a cocktail stick. Use paintbrush to apply glue around outside of clock face and to edge of biscuit. Wrap border around and trim to size, making sure join is at the top of the clock (12 o'clock).
4. *Loop.* Roll and indent a thin 8-cm snake of golden yellow for loop at the top of the watch and glue in place with tylose glue. Cover join with a strip of fondant, cut end into a v-shape and decorate with heart cutter.
5. *Crown.* Roll a 1-cm ball of golden yellow fondant and flatten. Make evenly spaced indents around side. Glue in place with tylose glue.

STAGE THREE

6. *Painting.* Mix gold lustre with decorator's spirit or vodka and paint yellow fondant golden, taking care not to get paint on clock face.

In humid weather or when a lot of colouring is used, such as for printing a photograph, the thin sheet of icing can stick to the backing and tear when removed. Cut your rounds and use a hairdryer to dry softened edible image sheets before attempting to remove clock faces.

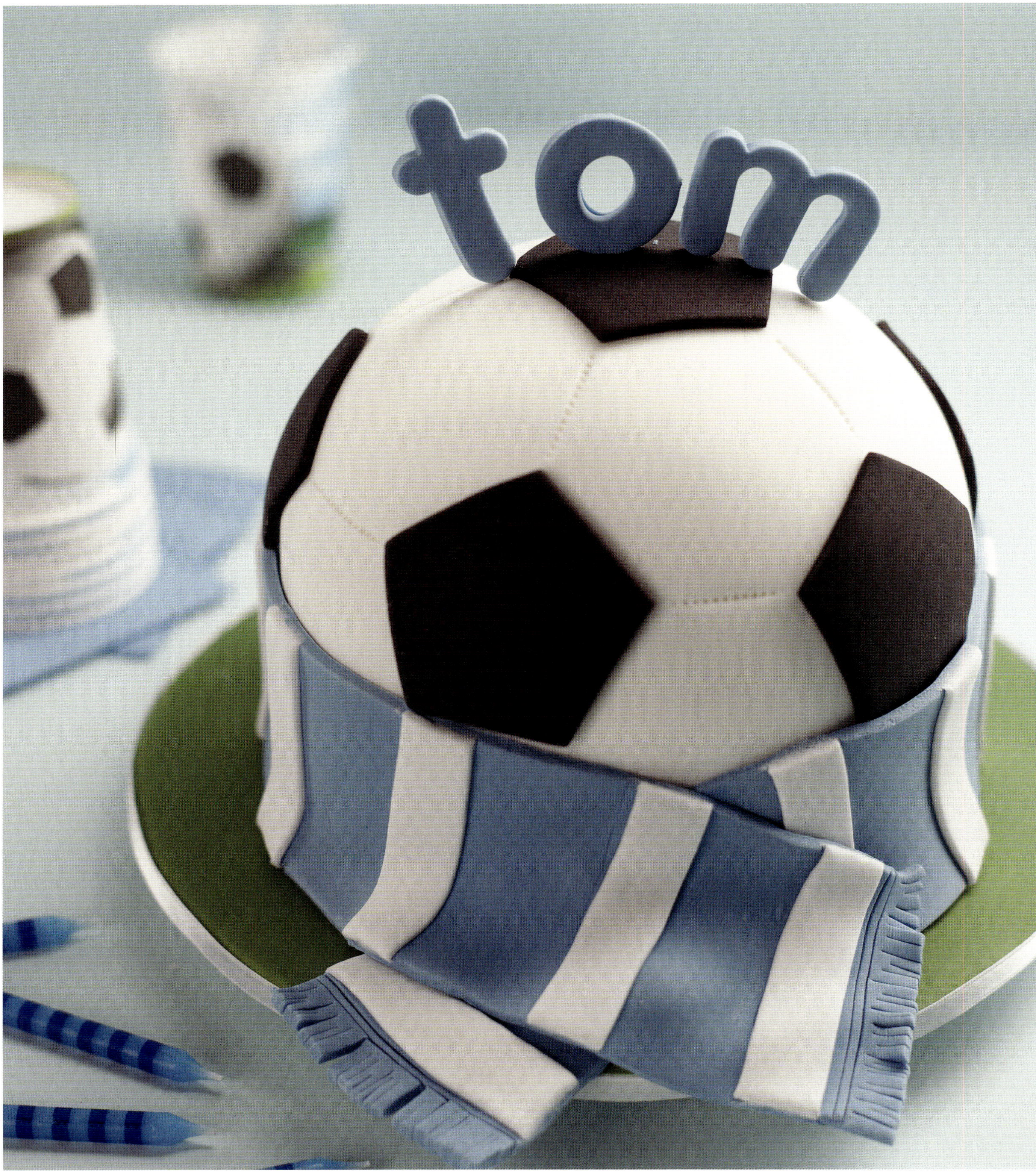
tom

it's a goal

Use the colours of a favourite team to make this cake a match winner with soccer players and fans.

CAKE REQUIREMENTS
- 1 x 15-cm (6") round cake (see pages 16–17)
- 1 x ball cake (see pages 16–17)

DECORATING INGREDIENTS
- 1 x ganache recipe (see page 13)
- 1 x apricot glaze recipe (see page 15)
- 2.95 kg fondant icing (pre-coloured store-bought or coloured with gel paste food colouring), set aside in plastic wrap
    - 1 kg white
    - 700 g green
    - 750 g blue
    - 500 g black
- pure icing sugar (for kneading)
- cornflour (for rolling out)
- tylose powder
- tylose glue (see page 15)

EQUIPMENT
- 25-cm (10") round heavy cake board
- 1 m white ribbon (10–15 mm wide)
- cake decorator's wire (number 20)
- pentagon template (see page 137)
- serrated knife
- large palette knife
- scraper with straight edge
- strip of cardboard from a milk carton (for smoothing curved ganache surface)
- pastry brush
- fine sieve (for sifting icing sugar when kneading)
- large and small rolling pins
- knife
- smoothers
- stitching tool
- lettering cutters
- small paintbrush (for applying tylose powder)
- ruler and measuring tape
- non-stick baking paper (for drying decorations)
- scissors
- non-toxic glue

cakestar 72

STAGE ONE

1. *Prepare cake.* Level both cakes, removing crust from top to give a flat surface, then fix ball cake on top of round cake using ganache. Use serrated knife to sculpt or correct shape wherever necessary. Secure cake to heavy board and cover with ganache (see page 19). Allow cake to set overnight, if possible.

STAGE TWO

2. *Cover cake.* Brush cake with apricot glaze and cover with kneaded white fondant. Smooth and trim off any excess fondant.
3. *Cover board.* The board can be covered at this stage or just before putting scarf on the cake. Knead green fondant and roll out large enough to cover board. Cut a 15-cm (6") round from the centre and lift fondant over cake and onto board, fixing with tylose glue and smoothing and trimming. Trim edge of board with ribbon, securing with non-toxic glue.
4. *Name.* Knead tylose powder (see page 15) into blue fondant. Roll out to 5 mm thick and cut out name of birthday person. Brush ends of short pieces of decorator's wire with tylose glue and insert into base of each letter. Allow to dry for several hours or overnight.
5. *Patterning.* Roll out black fondant and use pentagon template (see page 137) to cut 5 pieces. Use tylose glue to attach first of these to the centre of the top of cake. Add the next row of pentagons around cake, securing with tylose glue once you are happy with their positioning. Use a stitching tool or knife to mark lines out from each of the points to complete pattern. The pattern does not need to go all the way to the base of the cake as this will be covered by the scarf.

STAGE THREE

6. *Scarf.* To avoid cracking and marking, you need to work quickly when making the scarf. Roll out white fondant and cut 12 strips, 3 cm wide and 8 cm long. Cover with plastic wrap while you make main part of the scarf.
7. Roll out blue fondant to a strip 60 cm long by 8 cm wide. Use a knife to make small cuts at each end to form fringe.
8. Position white stripes so they are evenly spaced along scarf and glue into position with tylose glue. Trim any white strips that are too long.
9. *Wrap scarf around cake.* Brush lower part of soccer ball with tylose glue, carefully pick up scarf and wrap it around cake.
10. Position ends of scarf so they cross over and glue into position.

STAGE FOUR

11. *Finishing touches.* Once letters have set dry, position them on the cake by inserting wires down into cake.

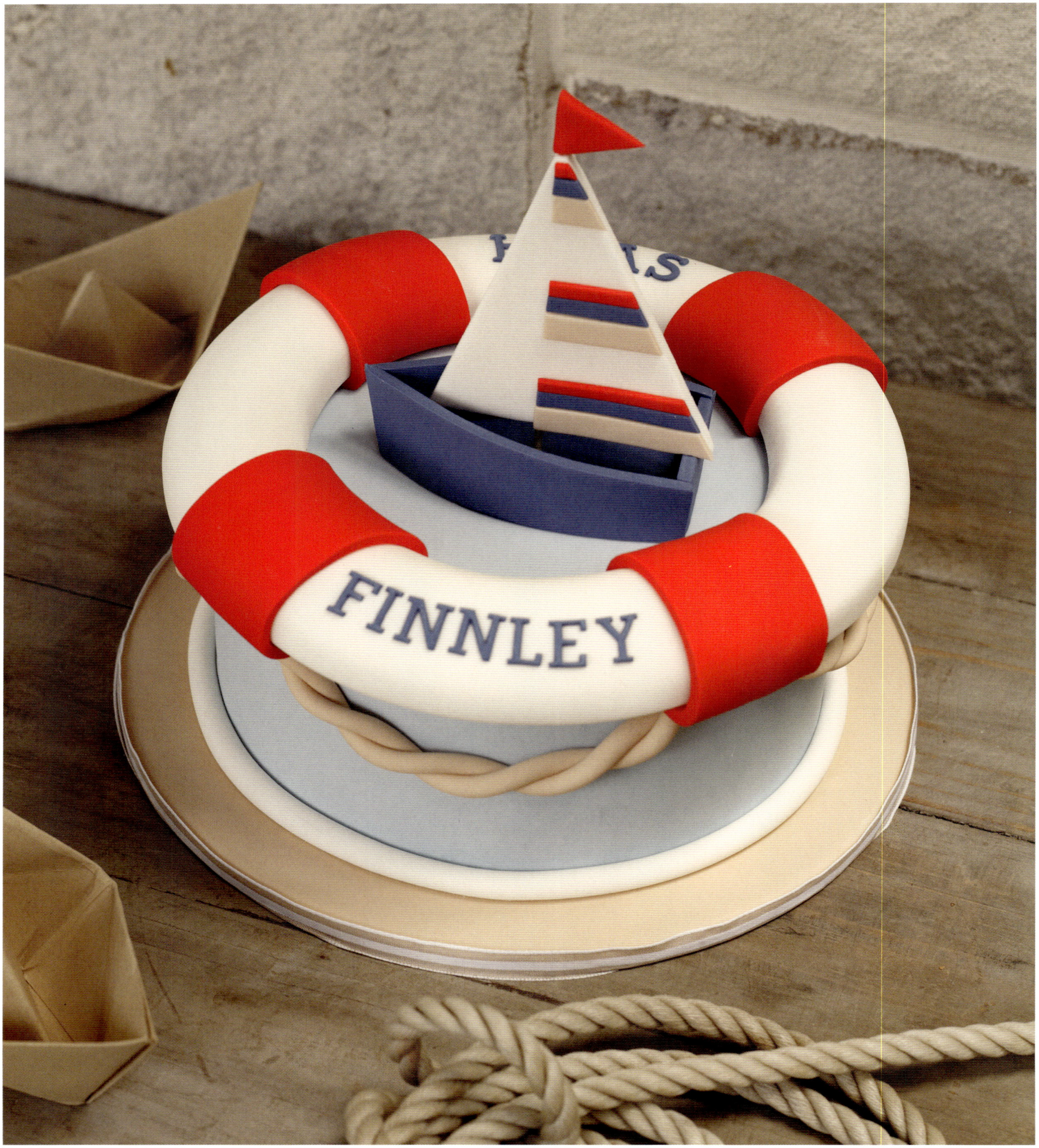
FINNLEY

setting sail

Red, white and blue, how I love you! With this classic colour palette you can set sail and get carried away with all things nautical.

CAKE REQUIREMENTS
- 1 x 20-cm (8") round cake (see pages 16–17)

DECORATING INGREDIENTS
- 1 x ganache recipe (see page 13)
- 1 x apricot glaze recipe (see page 15)
- 2.9 kg fondant icing (pre-coloured store-bought or coloured with gel paste food colouring), set aside in plastic wrap
    - 750 g taupe
    - 750 g white
    - 200 g navy blue
    - 800 g pale blue
    - 400 g red
- pure icing sugar (for kneading)
- cornflour (for rolling out)
- tylose powder
- tylose glue (see page 15)

EQUIPMENT
- 28-cm (11") round heavy cake board
- 1 m white or taupe ribbon (10–15 mm wide)
- 1 thin wooden kitchen skewer
- templates (see page 136)
- serrated knife
- large palette knife
- scraper with straight edge
- pastry brush
- fine sieve (for sifting icing sugar when kneading)
- large and small rolling pins
- knife
- lettering cutters
- ruler
- measuring tape
- smoothers
- small paintbrush (for applying tylose glue)
- non-stick baking paper (for drying decorations)
- scissors
- non-toxic glue

cakestar 76

STAGE ONE

1. *Prepare cake.* Level cake, removing crust from top to give a flat surface, and invert so trimmed surface becomes base of cake. Secure cake to heavy board and cover with ganache (see page 19). Allow cake to set overnight, if possible.

STAGE TWO

2. *Cover cake.* Brush cake with apricot glaze and cover with kneaded pale blue fondant rolled out to 3 mm thick. Smooth and trim off any excess fondant.
3. *Cover board.* Knead taupe fondant and roll out large enough to cover board. Cut out a 20-cm (8") round from the centre, lift over cake and onto board, fixing with tylose glue and smoothing and trimming. Roll a snake of white icing and glue around base of cake to conceal join between cake and board. Trim board with ribbon, securing with non-toxic glue.
4. *Boat.* Knead tylose powder (see page 15) into navy blue fondant and roll out to 3 mm thick. Use boat template and sharp knife to cut out 4 pieces that make up boat. Use tylose glue to attach sides and back of the boat to base piece.
5. *Sail.* Knead tylose powder (see page 15) into remaining white fondant. Roll out a piece of fondant to 5 mm thick, then use sail template and knife to cut out sail. Insert kitchen skewer through centre, leaving 1 cm of skewer poking out the top. Knead tylose powder into red fondant and use a small piece to cut a triangular flag. Fit this to top of sail by threading onto skewer. Cut stripes from thinly rolled blue, taupe and red fondant to decorate. Leave to dry several hours or overnight.
6. *Shape life ring.* Measure around outside of cake with string or a tape measure. Use white fondant to roll a thick sausage shape to same length, trimming ends neatly and flattening slightly with palms of your hands. Bend icing into a circle, using tylose glue to join ends.
7. *Decorate life ring.* Roll out red fondant to 3 mm thick. Use ruler and knife to cut 4 strips 5 cm x 14 cm. Stick first of these in position around the life ring to cover the join, then position the other 3 pieces at even intervals. Roll out navy blue fondant to 1 mm thick. Use lettering cutters to cut out your message and stick letters in place. Allow to dry for several hours or overnight. If you don't have lettering cutters, you can pipe letters with coloured royal icing.
8. *Ropes.* To make 4 sections of rope, roll 8 long sausages of taupe icing to around 5 mm thick. Working quickly to ensure the icing does not dry and crack, twist pairs together to form 4 ropes and trim to a length of 25 cm. Glue into position on cake with tylose glue – they must be evenly spaced to match the red bands on the life ring. Flatten where they meet at top of cake so the life ring will have a flat surface to rest on.

STAGE THREE

9. *Position life ring.* Lift life ring into position so red strips are above joins in rope sections. You will have to take care to support life ring well when lifting or it may crack. Glue in place using tylose glue.
10. *Assemble boat.* Use tylose glue to stick boat in the centre of life ring. The sail is positioned by pushing support skewer carefully through the base of boat and into cake.

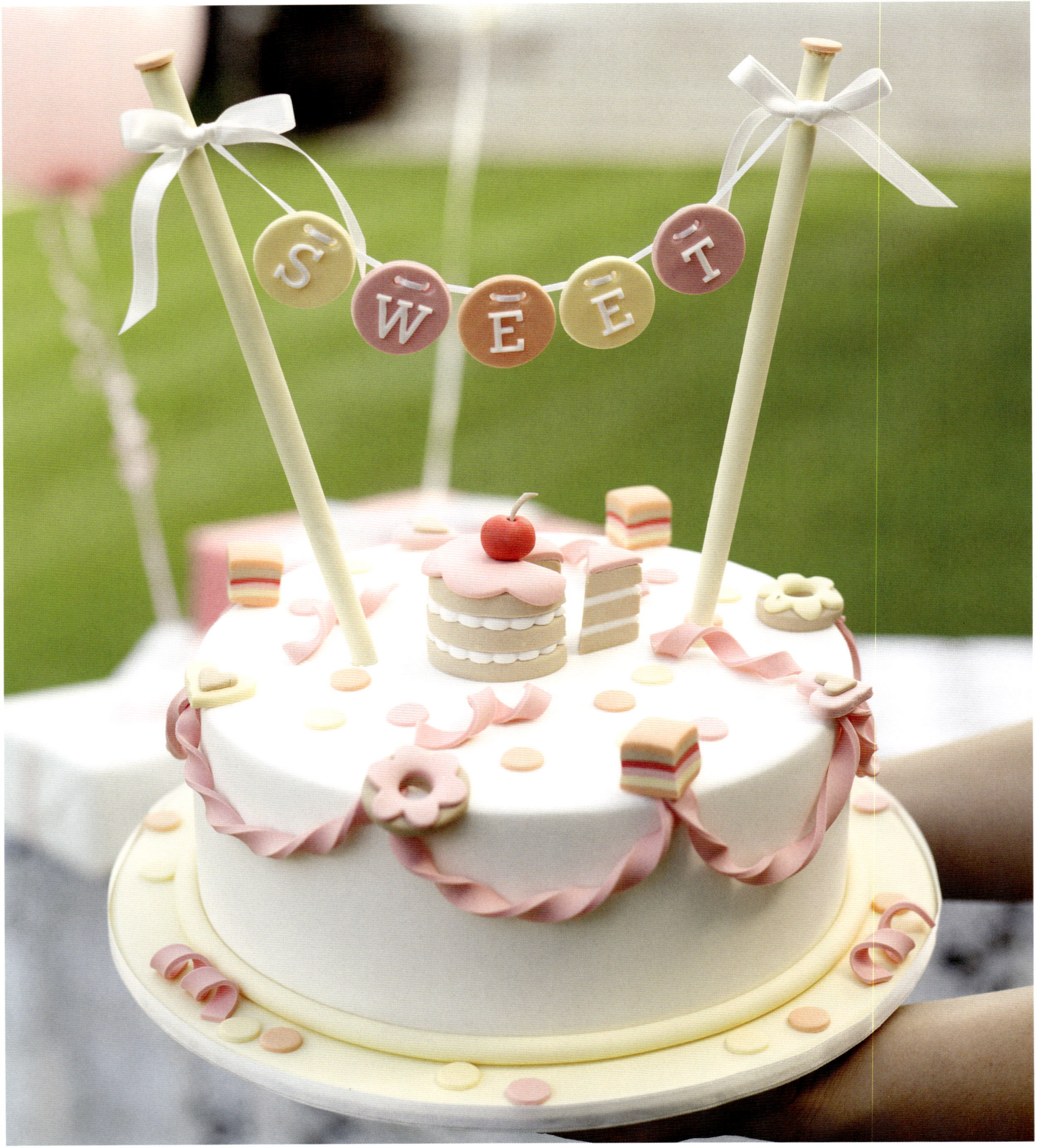
SWEET

sweets for the sweet

Edible bunting, confetti, streamers and all sorts of sugary sweet treats make this cake a party in itself. Change the colours and use the name of the birthday person.

CAKE REQUIREMENTS
- 1 x 23-cm (9") round cake (see pages 16–17)

DECORATING INGREDIENTS
- 1 x ganache recipe (see page 13)
- 1 x apricot glaze recipe (see page 15)
- 2.55 kg fondant icing (pre-coloured store-bought or coloured with gel paste food colouring), set aside in plastic wrap
    - 1.2 kg white
    - 900 g yellow
    - 50 g red
    - 100 g pink
    - 100 g orange
    - 200 g light brown
- pure icing sugar (for kneading)
- cornflour (for rolling out)
- tylose powder
- tylose glue (see page 15)

EQUIPMENT
- 30-cm (12") round heavy board
- 1.5 m white ribbon (10–15 mm wide)
- 50 cm white ribbon (2.5 mm wide)
- 2 thick wooden skewers
- serrated knife
- large palette knife
- scraper with straight edge
- pastry brush
- fine sieve (for sifting icing sugar when kneading)
- large and small rolling pins
- knife
- heart cutters
- flower cutter
- blossom cutter
- circle cutters
- number 2 piping tip
- lettering cutters
- ruler
- smoothers
- small paintbrush (for applying tylose glue)
- non-stick baking paper (for drying decorations)
- scissors
- non-toxic glue

To save time, go to a specialist lolly shop and select a range of beautiful pastel candies and sugar-dusted jellies rather than making your own. You could even make the bunting from paper.

cakestar 79

cakestar 80

STAGE ONE

1. *Prepare cake.* Level cake, removing crust from top to give a flat surface and invert so trimmed surface becomes base of cake. Secure cake to heavy board and cover with ganache (see page 19). Allow cake to set overnight, if possible.

STAGE TWO

2. *Cover cake.* Brush cake with apricot glaze and cover using kneaded white fondant. Smooth and trim off any excess fondant.
3. *Cover board.* Knead yellow fondant and roll out large enough to cover board. Cut a 20-cm (8") round from the centre, lift over cake and onto board, fixing with tylose glue and smoothing and trimming. Roll out a snake of yellow icing and, using tylose glue, place it around base of cake to conceal join between the cake and board. Trim board with 10–15-mm-wide white ribbon, securing with non-toxic glue.
4. *Posts.* Roll out yellow fondant to 3 mm thick, brush with tylose glue and use to roll around the skewers, trimming to size with a knife so there is around 5 cm of uncovered skewer at the base (this will be inserted into the cake). Smooth the join.
5. *Confetti.* Roll out yellow, pink and orange fondant and use piping tip or circle cutter with a 1-cm diameter to cut out several spots from each colour. Allow to dry.
6. *Bunting.* Knead tylose powder (see page 15) into pink, yellow and orange fondant and roll out to 3 mm thick. Use a 3.5-cm circle cutter to cut enough discs to spell out your message and a couple of extras in case of breakages. With a number 2 piping tip, make 2 holes at the top of each disc where ribbon will later be threaded. Roll out white fondant to 1 mm thick and use lettering cutters to cut out your message and stick in place on the icing discs. Allow to dry for several hours or overnight. If you don't have lettering cutters, you can pipe letters with royal icing.
7. *Streamers.* Roll out pink fondant to 3 mm thick. Use a knife and ruler to cut out 8 strips, 1 cm wide and 12 cm long. Working quickly to ensure icing does not dry and crack, twist each strip and attach to cake at even intervals using tylose glue. Cut additional shorter strips, twist and use to decorate cake board.
8. *Love heart lollies.* Roll out pink and yellow fondant to 5 mm thick. Using a 3-cm heart cutter, cut 2 pink hearts and 1 yellow heart. Roll brown fondant to 3 mm thick and cut 3 x 1.5-cm hearts. Stick these on top of the larger hearts. Allow to dry.
9. *Iced doughnuts.* Roll out brown fondant to 7 mm thick. Cut out 2 rounds using a 3.5-cm-diameter cutter. Cut a hole in the centre of these using a piping tip or circle cutter with a 1-cm diameter. Roll out pink and yellow fondant to 2 mm thick and use a 3.5-cm-diameter flower cutter to cut out 2 shapes, cutting a hole in the centre of each of these using the same piping tip or circle cutter with a 1-cm diameter. Glue in place.
10. *Mini cake.* Roll out brown fondant to 1 cm thick and cut 3 x 6-cm-diameter rounds. Roll out white fondant to 3 mm thick and cut out 2 rounds using a scalloped circle cutter with a 6-cm diameter. Sandwich together using tylose glue. Roll out pink fondant to 2 mm thick and cut out icing for top of cake using a 7-cm-diameter blossom cutter. Glue in place, smoothing down sides of mini cake a little. Use a knife to cut a small slice from the cake. For the cherry, roll a 1.5-cm ball of red icing. Indent slightly at the top and bottom. Knead tylose powder (see page 15) into a tiny piece of brown fondant and roll into a tapered stem for the cherry. Make a small hole in top of cherry with a cocktail stick and use tylose glue to position the stem.

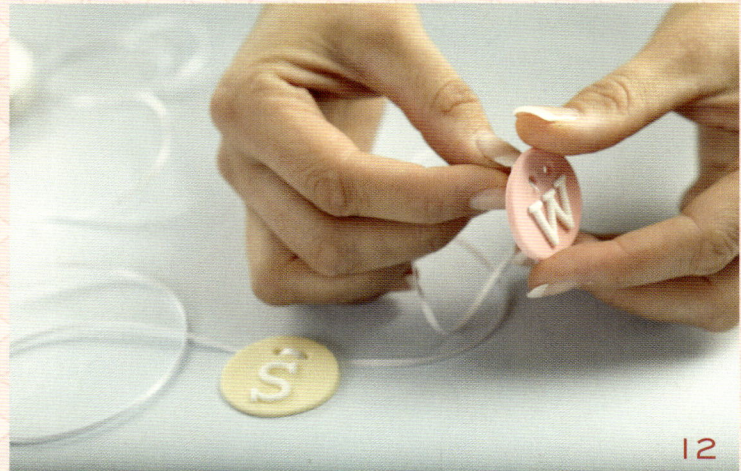

11. *Allsorts.* Roll out orange, yellow, pink, red and brown fondant to 3 mm thick. Sandwich together using tylose glue and use knife to cut into 2.5-cm squares.

STAGE THREE

12. *Assemble posts and bunting.* Once dry, thread bunting discs onto fine ribbon, tie each end around 2 cm from the top of the posts. Tie 2 bows with same width of ribbon used to trim the board and attach these with royal icing, allowing them to set a short while before standing up posts and inserting them into cake.
13. *Sweets.* Cover each join in the streamers around top edge of cake by gluing a sweet in place. Position cake and cake slice under bunting and glue in place. Scatter sugar confetti and extra streamers over surface of cake and cake board and glue in place once you are happy with their positioning.

cakestar 83

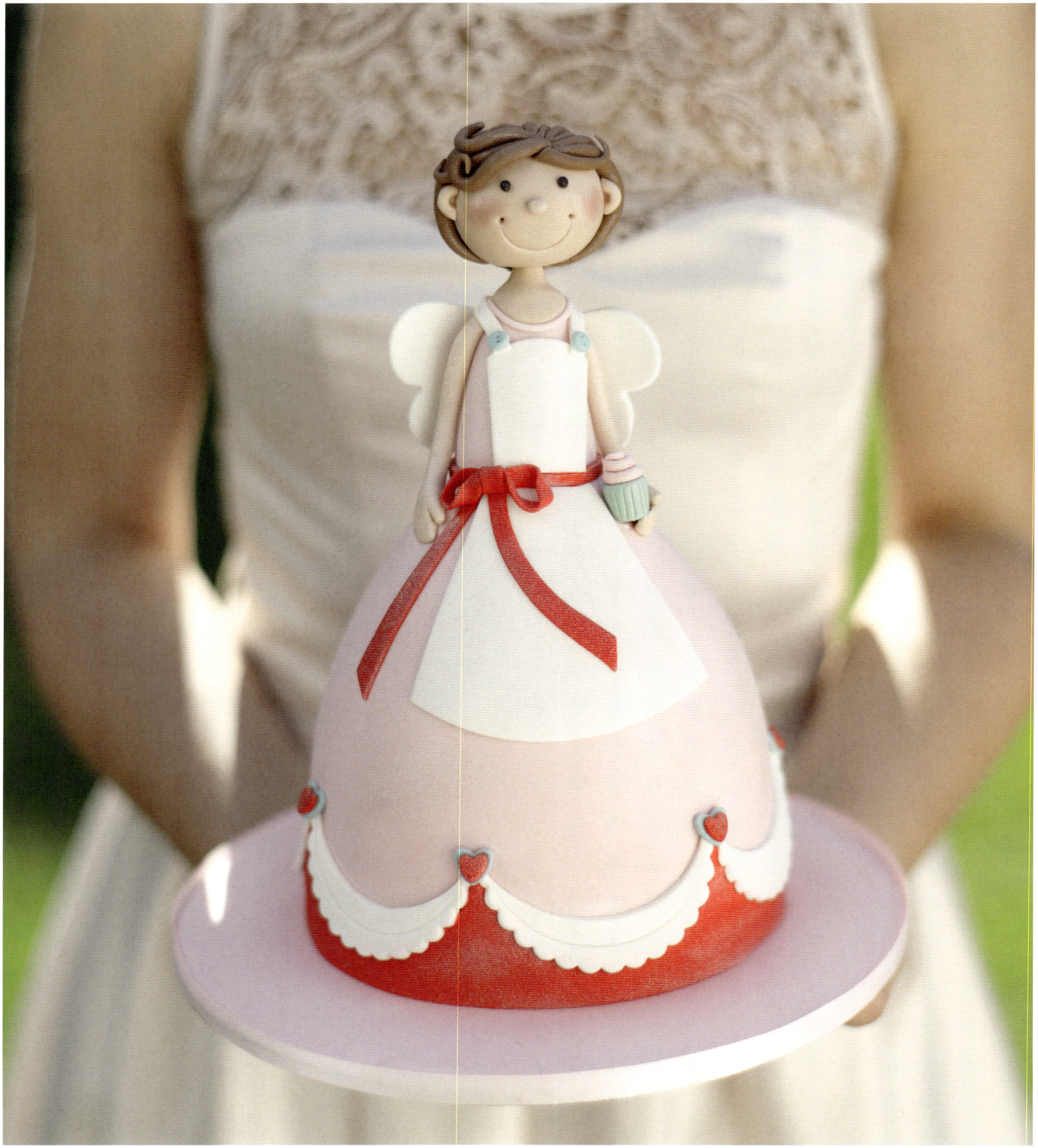

cake fairy

This beautiful fairy is a wish come true for any little girl. Change the colours and the detail on her dress and she can become a garden fairy, Christmas fairy or even a princess.

CAKE REQUIREMENTS

- 1 x 15-cm (6") round cake (see pages 16–17)
- 1 x small Dolly Varden cake

DECORATING INGREDIENTS

- 1 x ganache recipe (see page 13)
- 1 x apricot glaze recipe (see page 15)
- 2.8 kg fondant icing (pre-coloured store-bought or coloured with gel paste food colouring), set aside in plastic wrap
    - 1.8 kg pale pink
    - 300 g white
    - 400 g red
    - 150 g skin colour (made using pink, brown and yellow colours)
    - 30 g teal green
    - 5 g black
    - 80 g brown
- pure icing sugar (for kneading)
- cornflour (for rolling out)
- tylose powder
- tylose glue (see page 15)
- pink edible lustre

EQUIPMENT

- 25-cm (10") round heavy cake board
- 1 m pale pink ribbon (10–15 mm wide)
- 1 wooden kitchen skewer
- templates (see page 137)
- serrated knife
- large palette knife
- strip of cardboard (for smoothing curved ganache surface)
- pastry brush
- fine sieve (for sifting icing sugar when kneading)
- large and small rolling pins
- knife
- smoothers
- circle cutters
- scalloped circle cutters
- round piping tip (number 6)
- heart cutters (for skirt and wings)
- cocktail stick
- small paintbrush (for applying tylose glue)
- soft paintbrush
- small ball tool
- ruler
- non-toxic craft glue
- scissors

If you do not have a Dolly Varden tin, you can bake a high 15-cm (6") round cake and carve to shape.

To save time and effort you can leave off the apron and simplify the dress – she looks just as beautiful with a bow around her waist and sparkly cachous pressed into her skirt. She can also hold a birthday candle instead of making the tiny cupcake.

cakestar 86

STAGE ONE

1. *Prepare cake.* Level both cakes, removing crust from top of each to give a flat surface, then sandwich Dolly Varden cake on top of round cake using ganache. Use a serrated knife to sculpt or correct shape wherever necessary. Secure cake to heavy board and cover with ganache (see page 19). Allow cake to set overnight, if possible.

STAGE TWO

2. *Cover cake.* Brush cake with apricot glaze and cover in kneaded pale pink fondant. Smooth and trim off any excess fondant.
3. *Cover board.* Knead remaining pale pink fondant and roll out a piece large enough to cover board. Cut a 15-cm (6") round from the centre, lift fondant over cake and onto board, fixing with tylose glue and smoothing and trimming. Trim edge of board with pale pink ribbon, using non-toxic glue to fasten.
4. *Body.* Knead tylose powder (see page 15) into remaining pink fondant, roll into a ball and use smoother to shape into a slightly conical sausage. Cut thicker end to size with a knife and flatten on your work bench. Glue in place on skirt and insert a kitchen skewer through body and into skirt section, leaving 4 cm of skewer showing to support the head later.
5. *Head.* Roll skin-coloured fondant into a ball with a diameter of around 4 cm, flatten slightly and use kitchen skewer to make a hole at the base where it will fit onto the neck. While fondant is still soft, indent the smile using a small circle cutter and cocktail stick. The ears are made by rolling a tiny ball of skin-coloured fondant, indenting with a small ball tool and cutting in half, then stick in place with tylose glue. The nose is a tiny ball of skin-coloured fondant. Roll 2 tiny balls of black fondant and glue in place as eyes.
6. *Neck.* Knead tylose powder (see page 15) into skin-coloured fondant. Roll a small ball of fondant, then work between your hands to lengthen one end to form the neck, flattening the other to a circular shape to be shoulders and chest. Thread over skewer, glue in place and use fingers to smooth and neaten where it meets the dress. Roll a thin sausage of pink fondant to cover the join between neck and dress. Use knife to trim top of neck to correct height.
7. Allow head to dry a little while decorating the skirt section.

STAGE THREE

8. *Decorate skirt.* Add tylose powder (see page 15) to red fondant to make it more manageable to use. Roll out to 3 mm thick. Cut a 4-cm-wide strip long enough to reach around the circumference of the skirt. Use a 7-cm circle cutter to cut out evenly spaced semicircles and wrap around base of skirt, using tylose glue to stick in place. Roll out white fondant to 3 mm thick and use a frilled cutter (the same size as the circle cutter used to cut the red icing) to cut rounds. Cut these in half and use a slightly larger circle cutter to indent and cut out a curved section. Stick in place to conceal join between red detail and pink skirt. Cut out little hearts from thinly rolled teal and red fondant to decorate each peak at base of the skirt and stick in place with tylose glue.
9. *Apron.* Roll out white fondant to 3 mm thick. Use templates from page 137 and knife to cut apron top and bottom pieces and stick into place using tylose glue. Use red fondant containing tylose powder to make a strip around the waist of the fairy. Make and attach a small bow using the instructions on page 127.
10. *Wings.* Cut 2 hearts (4 cm wide) from white fondant strengthened with tylose powder and rolled out to 3 mm thick, and glue in place as wings.
11. *Head.* Apply pink lustre powder to the cheeks with a soft paintbrush. Brush tylose glue on the top of the neck and then put the head in place.

12

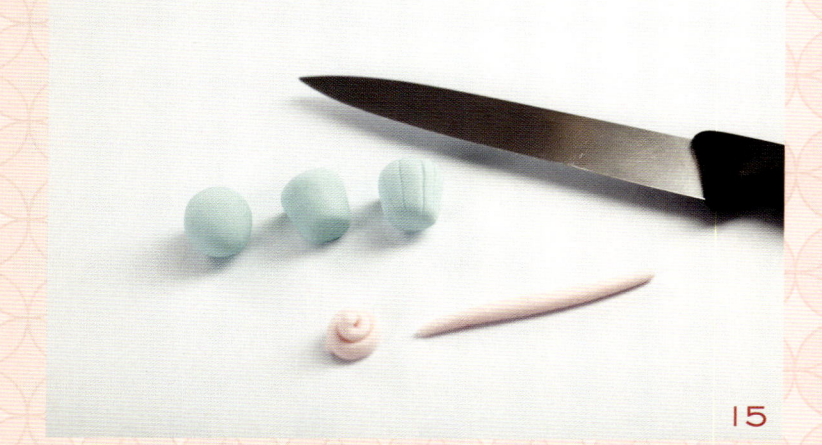

14

15

12. *Arms.* Roll skin-coloured fondant into a long sausage shape and cut in half. Indent slightly where the elbow and wrist will be and flatten hands. Use a knife to cut out a small 'v' shape between thumb and fingers. Glue in place at shoulders, bending and sticking in position.
13. *Apron straps and buttons.* Use a ruler and knife to cut 2 narrow strips of thinly rolled white fondant, attaching at the front of the apron and extending over the shoulders to the back, where they can be trimmed and glued in place. The buttons are made by cutting 2 tiny rounds of teal fondant with a piping tip and marking the holes in the buttons with a cocktail stick.

STAGE FOUR

14. *Hair.* Roll tapered pieces of brown fondant to form the hair, gluing in position, starting in the centre of the head and working out to each side. Roll smaller pieces, curling one end as the fairy's fringe.
15. *Cupcake.* For the base of the cupcake roll a 1.5-cm ball of teal fondant, flattening into a slightly conical shape. Indent lines using a knife. Roll a small tapered snake of pink fondant and curl to form frosting on cupcake. Glue together and then glue in position in the fairy's hand.

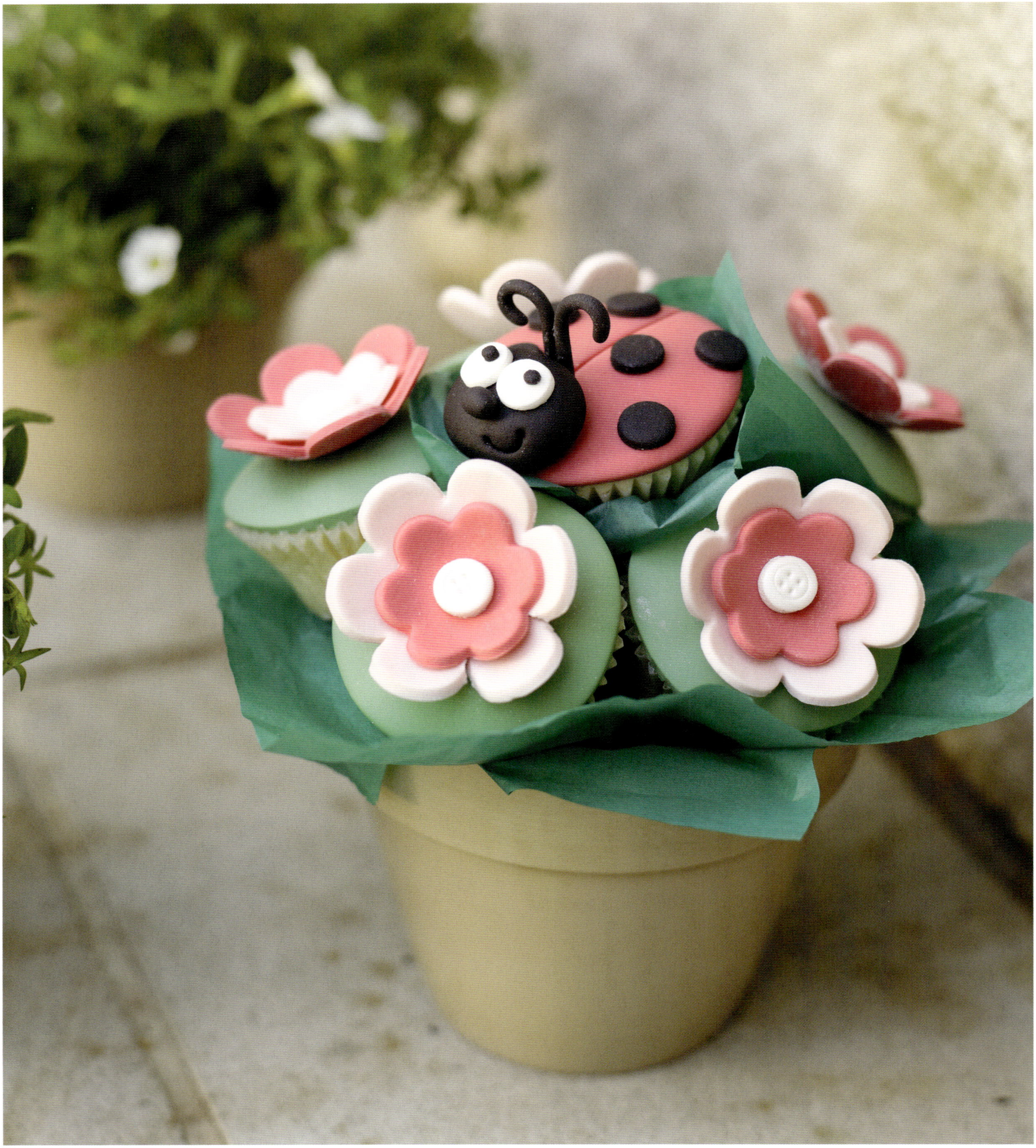

cute as a button bouquet

Cute as a button, or perhaps even more cute than a ladybug's ear, a bouquet of cupcakes is a beautiful gift.

CAKE REQUIREMENTS

- 6 large cupcakes (see pages 16–17)

DECORATING INGREDIENTS

- ½ x buttercream recipe (see page 13)
- ½ x royal icing recipe (see page 14)
- 780 g fondant icing (pre-coloured store-bought or coloured with gel paste food colouring), set aside in plastic wrap
    - 350 g green
    - 200 g watermelon (deep pink with a touch of red)
    - 150 g pale pink
    - 40 g white
    - 40 g black
- pure icing sugar (for kneading)
- cornflour (for rolling out)
- tylose powder
- tylose glue (see page 15)

EQUIPMENT

- florist foam
- small clay pot (around 15 cm diameter)
- green tissue paper
- 6 candy sticks
- small palette knife
- fine sieve (for sifting icing sugar when kneading)
- small rolling pin
- smoother
- knife
- circle cutters and round piping tips
- medium and large flower cutters
- small paintbrush (for applying tylose glue)
- piping bag and couplers
- number 2 piping tip
- tray (for drying flowers)
- cocktail sticks
- scissors

cakestar 92

STAGE ONE

1. *Icing floral cupcakes*. Coat 5 cupcakes in buttercream icing then fondant-ice in green (see page 21).
2. *Flowers*. Knead tylose powder (see page 15) into watermelon and pink fondant. On a surface dusted with cornflour, roll out watermelon fondant to a very thin, even thickness and cut 3 large flowers and 3 small flowers. Dust a flower drying tray or rounded cupcake tray with cornflour and place flowers in to dry. Repeat with pale pink fondant. (This gives one spare flower in case of a breakage.)
3. *Button centres*. Knead tylose powder (see page 15) into white fondant. Roll out to 5 mm thick. Cut 1-cm rounds for each of the 5 flower cupcakes, indent an inner round using a slightly smaller cutter or large round piping tip. Mark buttonholes by indenting with a cocktail stick. Allow flowers to dry while you work on ladybug cupcake.

STAGE TWO

4. *Icing ladybug cupcake*. Coat remaining cupcake in buttercream icing then fondant-ice in watermelon (see page 21). While fondant is still soft, use knife to indent a line down centre of cupcake.
5. *Spots*. Roll out black fondant to a thin, even thickness. Use a 1-cm piping tip or circle cutter to cut spots for ladybug and a small piping tip to cut 2 tiny rounds for pupils. Position larger spots randomly on the cupcake, using tylose glue. Keep pupils aside.
6. *Ladybug face*. Knead tylose powder (see page 15) into remaining black fondant. Roll a 2.5-cm ball of fondant and flatten slightly. Use edge of a piping tip or small circle cutter to indent mouth, marking each end with a cocktail stick. The antennae are 2 small tapered snakes and nose is a very small ball rolled into an oval shape. Eyes are cut with the 1-cm round cutter from thinly rolled white fondant. Assemble face, then secure face and antennae in place on cupcake with tylose glue. Allow to set before arranging in bouquet.
7. *Assemble flower cupcakes*. Use royal icing to stick large flower onto top of each cupcake, with another dot of icing holding smaller flower and then centre in place. Allow to set before arranging in bouquet.

cakestar 94

STAGE THREE

8. *Arrangement.* Cut florist foam to fit snugly in the base of the pot. Cover with offset sheets of green tissue. Beginning with outer row, position cupcakes by first inserting a candy stick through paper and into foam and carefully pressing cupcake onto this so the stick goes about 2 cm through base of cupcake. If it is too difficult to push stick through base, you can make a small piercing in cupcake wrapper with a sharp knife. Apply a generous dot of royal icing where cupcake wrapper meets candy stick to secure. Once 5 outer cupcakes are in position, wrap ladybug cupcake in an extra layer of paper for added greenery and put into position in the same way.

9. *Storage.* If you are not serving cupcakes immediately, allow royal icing to set, then wrap bouquet in cellophane to keep fresh.

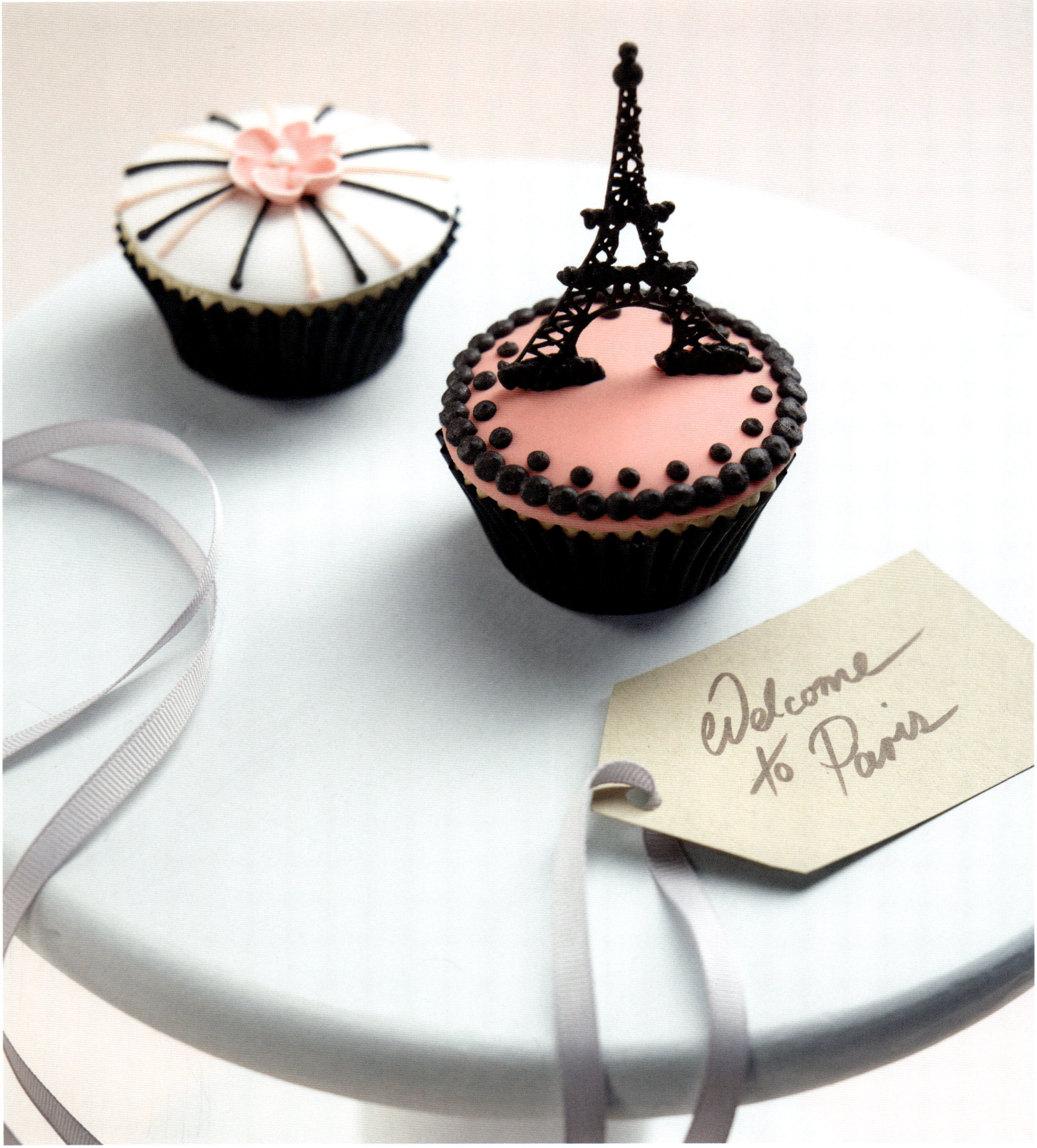
Welcome
to Paris

we'll always have paris

These ornate and fanciful cupcakes are a decadent treat for lovers of the City of Lights. The delicate silhouette of the Eiffel Tower and the striped skirts of cancan dancers bring Paris style to your soirée. Makes 16.

CAKE REQUIREMENTS

- 16 medium cupcakes (see pages 16–17)

DECORATING INGREDIENTS

- ½ x buttercream recipe (see page 13)
- 1 x royal icing recipe (see page 14)
- black and pink food colouring
- 800 g fondant icing (pre-coloured store-bought or coloured with gel paste food colouring), set aside in plastic wrap
    - 400 g white
    - 400 g pink
- pure icing sugar (for kneading)
- cornflour (for rolling out)
- 8 sugar flowers (we used Queen Icing Flowers)

EQUIPMENT

- non-stick baking paper
- small palette knife
- fine sieve (for sifting icing sugar when kneading)
- small rolling pin
- circle cutters
- template (see page 137)
- 2 piping bags
- 2 couplers
- 2 x number 2 piping tips
- 1 x number 1 piping tip
- small paintbrush
- dressmaker's pins

Timing is key. It is essential that the Eiffel Towers have at least 24 hours to dry before you attempt to remove them from the baking paper. It is a good idea to make the Eiffel Towers the day before you bake your cupcakes. That way they will have set hard enough to handle by the time your cupcakes are cooled and ready to decorate.

cakestar 98

STAGE ONE

1. *Eiffel Towers.* Using template on page 137, trace outline onto a piece of white paper. Cut a square of non-stick baking paper and place over outline. Mix half the royal icing with black food colouring and place in a piping bag fitted with a number 2 tip. Pipe vertical lines of tower, then archway. Swap to a number 1 tip to fill in spaces with a zigzag design before adding wavy cross pieces and dots at top using the number 2 tip. Carefully move template under baking paper to a new position and pipe your next tower. Repeat process. You need 8, but pipe extra towers in case of breakages. Let completed towers sit undisturbed (movement of paper will cause them to crack when they are not dried) for at least 24 hours.

STAGE TWO

2. *Icing cupcakes.* Coat cupcakes in buttercream icing then fondant-ice 8 in white and 8 in pink (see page 21).

STAGE THREE

3. *Piping striped cancan design on white cupcakes.* Mix remaining royal icing with pink food colouring and place in a piping bag. With pink and black piping bags fitted with number 2 piping tips, begin by first piping black lines at equal intervals and then adding pink lines between these. Pipe from one side of cupcake, up and over centre to the other side. While royal icing is still soft, place a store-bought sugar flower in the centre.

4. *Piping spots and squiggle designs on pink cupcakes.* With black piping bag still fitted with a number 2 piping tip, pipe outside row of spots first, piping several and then flattening any peaks of icing with a slightly damp paintbrush before moving on. Add inner dots at equal intervals. For the squiggle cupcakes, use the same number 2 piping tip and pipe squiggly lines in random patterns.

5. *Position Eiffel Towers.* Carefully bend paper under each tower and they should lift off. Some breakages are unavoidable. Use black royal icing on base of tower to attach to top of each pink cupcake, holding in position with a dressmaker's pin while it dries.

Have a piece of slightly damp paper towel beside you when you work and wrap unused piping tip in this to prevent the icing drying and crusting before you use it next.

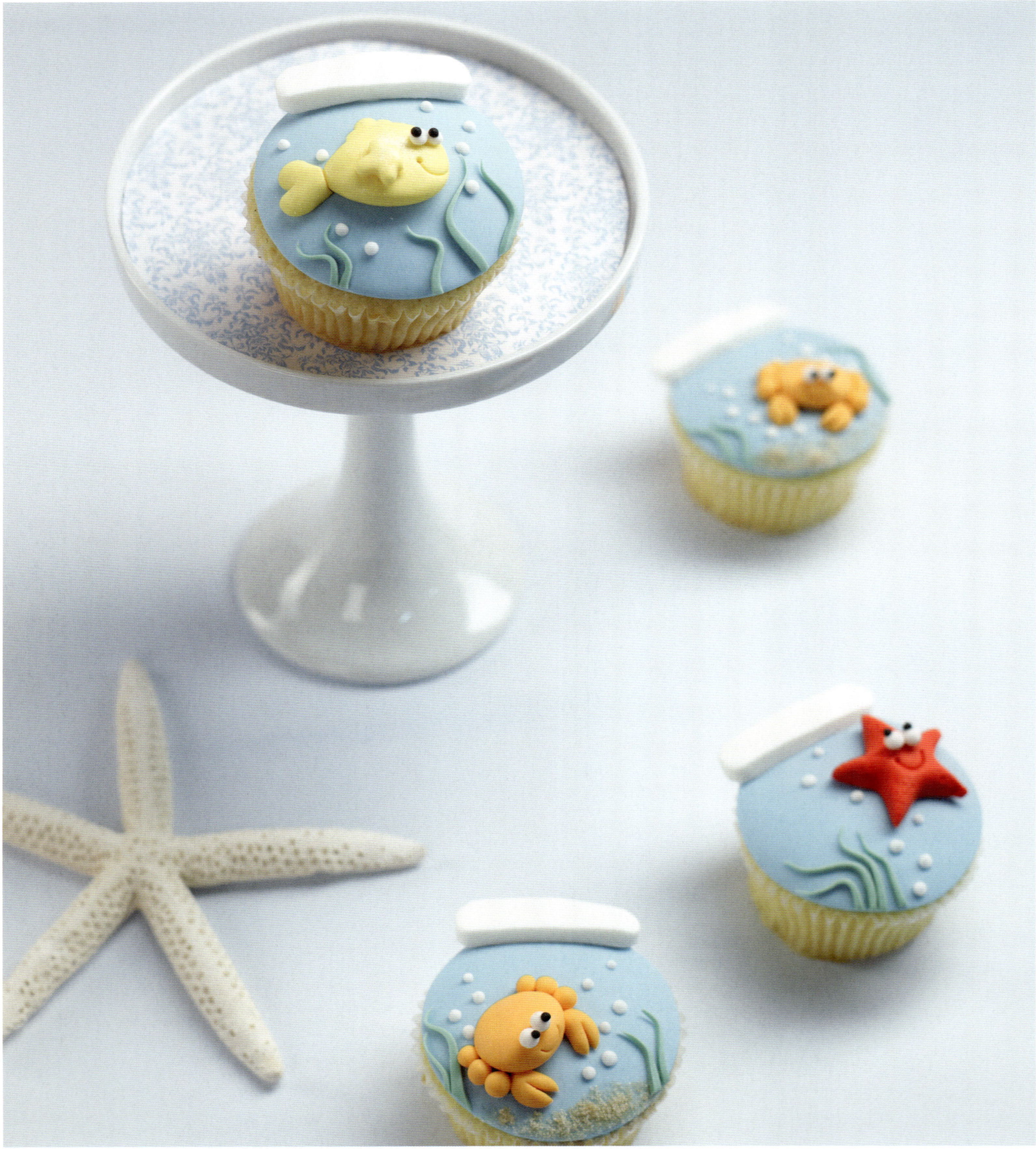

cupcake aquariums

These little fish bowls are perfect for an under-the-sea, mermaid or beach-themed party. If you are short on time, use store-bought lolly fish. Makes 12.

CAKE REQUIREMENTS

- 12 large cupcakes (see pages 16–17)

DECORATING INGREDIENTS

- ½ x buttercream recipe (see page 13)
- ½ x royal icing recipe (see page 14)
- 1.7 kg fondant icing (pre-coloured store-bought or coloured with gel paste food colouring), set aside in plastic wrap
    - 750 g pale blue
    - 300 g white
    - 100 g green
    - 150 g red
    - 100 g black
    - 150 g orange
    - 150 g yellow
- pure icing sugar (for kneading)
- cornflour (for rolling out)
- 1 tbsp brown sugar
- 1 tbsp caster sugar
- 1 tbsp raw sugar
- tylose glue (see page 15)

EQUIPMENT

- small palette knife
- small rolling pin
- knife
- smoother
- circle cutters
- ruler
- small paintbrush (for applying tylose glue)
- star cutter (4 cm wide)
- Dresden tool
- number 2 piping tip
- coupler and piping bag

cakestar 102

STAGE ONE

1. *Icing cupcakes.* Coat cupcakes in buttercream icing and then fondant-ice in pale blue (see page 21).

STAGE TWO

2. *Sand.* Combine brown sugar, caster sugar and raw sugar on a small plate to make a sandy consistency. Use paintbrush to apply tylose glue across what will be the base of each 'fishbowl', taking care to glue only where you would like sand to stick. Carefully press glued section into sandy mixture.
3. *Top rim.* Roll out white fondant to 5 mm thick. Use ruler and knife to cut into strips 5 cm long by 1.5 cm wide, rounding edges slightly. Stick in place across top of the cupcake using tylose glue to form the rim of fish bowl.
4. *Seaweed.* Roll out green icing to 3 mm thick, using knife to cut thin tapered slices. Glue into position at bottom of cupcakes, bending and positioning each piece differently so they look natural.
5. *Bubbles.* Use a piping tube filled with white royal icing and fitted with a number 2 tip, pipe small dots of various sizes to represent bubbles rising to the surface. Flatten any pointed tips of icing with a damp paintbrush.

STAGE THREE

6. *Starfish (makes 4).* Roll out red fondant to 1 cm thick and use the star cutter to cut out each body. While fondant is still soft, pinch with your fingers to curve edges and indent mouth with a small circle cutter or end of a piping tube, making a tiny dot at each end with a cocktail stick. Create a pattern along each arm using number 2 tip to indent tiny rounds. Roll balls of white fondant as eyeballs and smaller balls of black fondant as pupils. Use tylose glue to assemble.
7. *Crab (makes 4).* To make each body, roll 10 g orange fondant into a ball, flattening slightly between your hands. Indent mouth with a small circle cutter or end of a piping tube. For legs of each crab, roll 6 tiny balls of orange fondant, with front legs being slightly larger than back legs. Each claw is made using a ball of icing elongated and then cut with a knife and opened slightly. Roll tiny balls of white fondant for eyeballs and smaller balls of black fondant for pupils. Use tylose glue to assemble.
8. *Fish (makes 4).* To make each body, roll 10 g yellow icing into a ball, working one end of this between your hands to lengthen and narrow into a fat teardrop shape. Flatten slightly by pressing between your hands. The tail and fins are formed from smaller balls of fondant rolled into teardrop shapes, flattened and indented using a Dresden tool. Roll tiny balls of white fondant for eyeballs and smaller balls of black fondant for pupils. Use tylose glue to assemble.

STAGE FOUR

9. *Assemble.* Attach sea creatures to cupcakes using tylose glue.

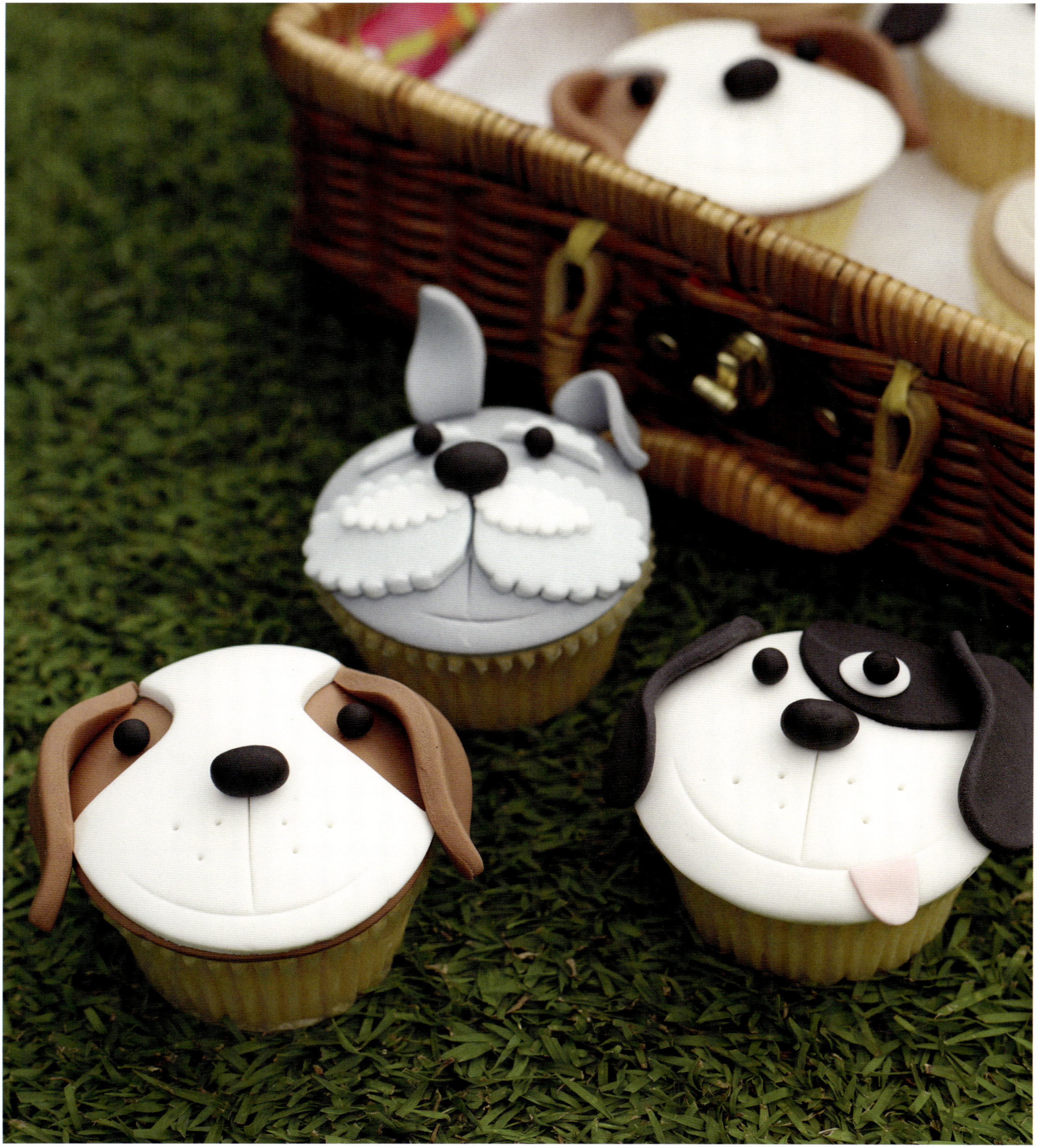

puppy love

These are inspired by three much-loved puppies – Suki Schafferman, Chloe Lipton and Bobo Batchellor. Alter the design and colours to make your pet. Makes 12.

CAKE REQUIREMENTS

- 12 large cupcakes (see pages 16–17)

DECORATING INGREDIENTS

- ½ x buttercream recipe (see page 13)
- 1.25 kg fondant icing (pre-coloured store-bought or coloured with gel paste food colouring), set aside in plastic wrap
    - 250 g brown
    - 425 g white
    - 250 g black
    - 300 g grey
    - 20 g pink
- pure icing sugar (for kneading)
- cornflour (for rolling out)
- tylose powder
- tylose glue (see page 15)
- 1 piece dried spaghetti

EQUIPMENT

- templates (see page 136)
- small palette knife
- fine sieve (for sifting icing sugar when kneading)
- small rolling pin
- smoother
- knife
- circle cutters and round piping tips
- scalloped circle cutters
- small paintbrush (for applying tylose glue)
- cocktail sticks

SUGAR SUKI

CANDY CHLOE

ICED BOBO

cakestar 106

sugar suki
Makes 4

STAGE ONE
1. *Icing cupcakes.* Coat 4 cupcakes in buttercream icing then fondant-ice in brown (see page 21).

STAGE TWO
2. *Muzzle.* Roll out white fondant to 3 mm thick. Using the same circle cutter as used to cover the cupcakes, cut a round of white for each face. Overlay Suki face template (see page 136) and use a knife to cut shape into each round of fondant. Use a circle cutter to indent mouths, a knife to mark centre line and cocktail stick to indent whiskers. Stick in place on cupcake with tylose glue.
3. *Nose and eyes.* Roll 2 tiny black balls for eyes of each puppy and a larger elongated ball for each nose. Attach with tylose glue.
4. *Ears.* Knead tylose powder (see page 15) into remaining brown fondant, roll out to 3 mm thick and cut 2 ears for each puppy using Suki ear template (see page 136), bend to give them shape and stick in place with tylose glue.

candy chloe
Makes 4

STAGE ONE
1. *Icing cupcakes.* Coat 4 cupcakes in buttercream icing then fondant-ice in grey (see page 21). While fondant is still soft, use a circle cutter to indent mouths and a knife to mark centre lines.

STAGE TWO
2. *Muzzle.* Add 75 g white fondant to remaining grey to lighten slightly. Roll out pale grey fondant and use a 4-cm scalloped circle cutter to cut 3 rounds for each puppy. Roll out white fondant and use same cutter to cut a white round for each puppy, then cut off 2 portions with cutter to give oval shapes. Position white pieces on 2 of the grey, trimming a narrow piece from side as pictured so they can be positioned close together on the cupcake to make up the muzzle of each dog. Cut 2 narrow eyebrow pieces from the third grey round and stick in place on each puppy using tylose glue.
3. *Nose and eyes.* Roll 2 tiny black balls for eyes of each puppy and a larger elongated ball for nose. Attach with tylose glue.
4. *Ears.* Knead tylose powder (see page 15) into remaining grey fondant, roll out to 3 mm thick and cut 2 ears for each puppy using Chloe ear template (see page 136). Insert a piece of spaghetti into one to give support and bend other to give shape. Stick in place with tylose glue.

iced bobo
Makes 4

STAGE ONE
1. *Icing cupcakes.* Coat 4 cupcakes in buttercream icing then fondant-ice in white (see page 21). While fondant is still soft, use a circle cutter to indent mouths, a knife to mark centre line and a cocktail stick to make whiskers.

STAGE TWO
2. *Patch.* Roll out black fondant and use a 3-cm circle cutter to cut a patch for each puppy, trimming a little from one side where it will meet the side of cupcake with same circle cutter used to ice the cupcakes. Stick in place using tylose glue. Roll out white fondant, cut a 1-cm round for each puppy and position this on each patch.
3. *Tongue.* Thinly roll out pink icing, cut a 1-cm round for each tongue, elongate with a rolling pin and trim to size with a knife. Stick in place with tylose glue.
4. *Nose and eyes.* Roll 2 tiny black balls for eyes of each puppy and a larger elongated ball for nose. Attach with tylose glue.
5. *Ears.* Knead tylose powder (see page 15) into remaining black fondant, roll out and cut 2 ears for each puppy using Bobo ear template (see page 136), bend to give shape and stick in place with tylose glue.

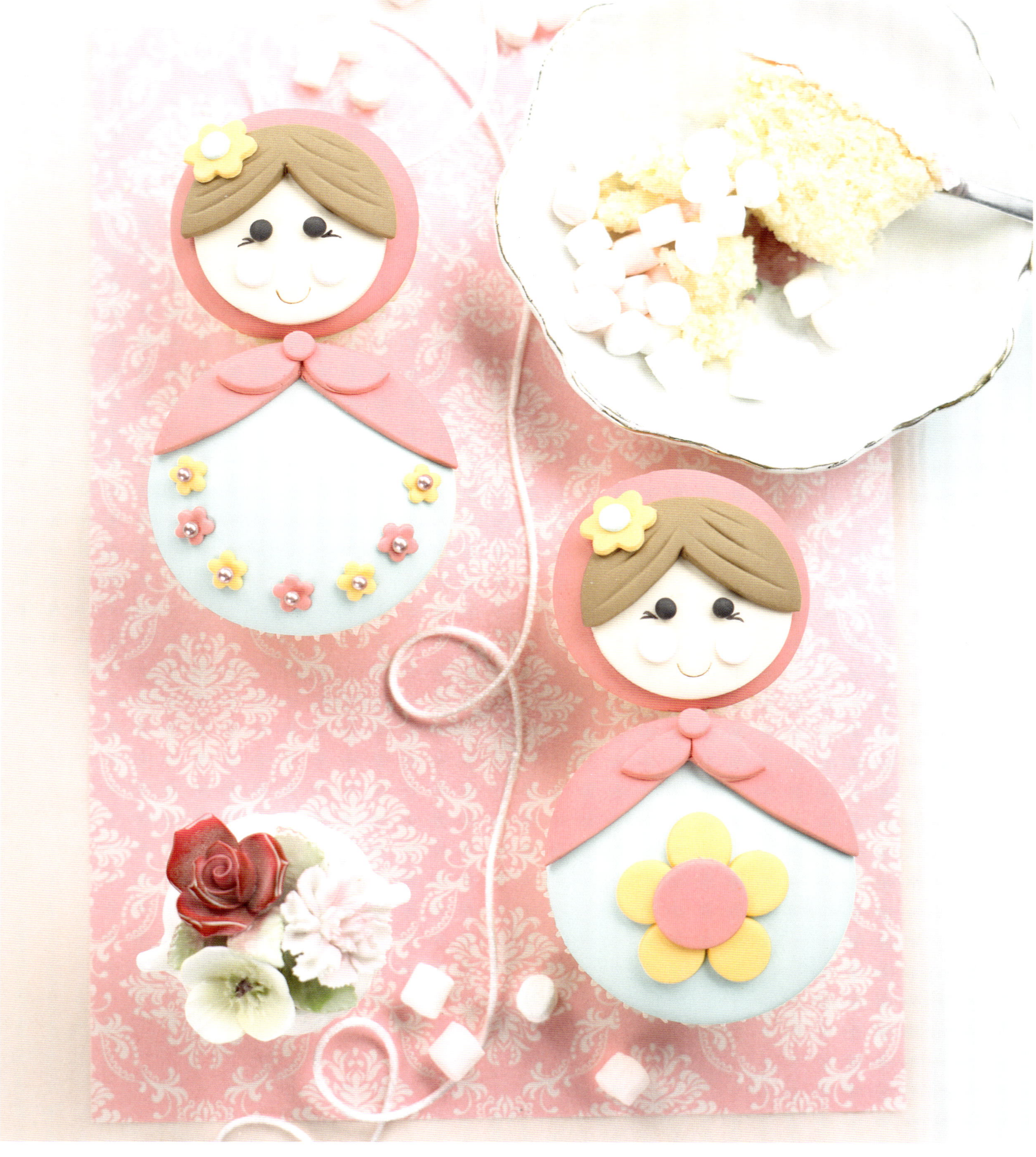

oh! babushka

Almost every little girl has had a set of Russian matroyshka dolls in their bedroom. Their rosy cheeks, colourful headscarves and patterned aprons are so cute on these little cupcakes and leave lots of scope to use your imagination when decorating them. My daughter collects Kimmidolls and I alter the colouring, hairstyle and add kimono arms to make little Japanese-inspired versions of these cakes for her. Makes 6.

CAKE REQUIREMENTS
- 6 medium cupcakes (see pages 16–17)
- 6 large cupcakes (see pages 16–17)

DECORATING INGREDIENTS
- 1 x buttercream recipe (see page 13)
- 1.4 kg fondant icing (pre-coloured store-bought or coloured with gel paste food colouring), set aside in plastic wrap
    - 450 g deep pink
    - 450 g teal blue
    - 200 g skin colour (made using pink, brown and yellow pastes)
    - 90 g brown
    - 150 g orange
    - 50 g pale pink
- pure icing sugar (for kneading)
- cornflour (for rolling out)
- tylose powder
- tylose glue (see page 15)

EQUIPMENT
- small palette knife
- fine sieve (for sifting icing sugar when kneading)
- small rolling pin
- knife
- smoother
- circle cutters and round piping tips
- blossom cutters
- Dresden tool
- black food-colouring pen
- small paintbrush (for applying tylose glue)
- 6 candy sticks

STAGE ONE

1. *Icing cupcakes.* Coat cupcakes in buttercream icing and then fondant-ice medium cupcakes in deep pink and large cupcakes in teal blue (see page 21).
2. *Face.* Roll out skin-coloured fondant icing to 3 mm thick and cut a round using a 5-cm circle cutter for each doll. Use tylose glue to stick in place on each medium cupcake, just below centre. Use edge of a small circle cutter or end of a piping tip to indent a mouth. Use 5-cm circle cutter to cut a brown round and, using a knife, cut this to form hair. Add texture using Dresden tool and stick in place. Roll 2 tiny black balls for eyes for each and use small circle cutter or large piping tip to cut pale pink cheeks for each face and glue all in place. Cut small blossoms from orange fondant and adhere to hair. Add eyelashes using a black food-colouring pen.
3. *Body.* For each doll, using same circle cutter used to fondant-ice large cupcakes, cut a round of deep pink, trim to shape with a knife to become bottom half of the scarf, cut a 2.5-cm round of pink icing, divide this in half to become ties on the scarf. A small flattened ball of icing forms the knot. Stick in place using tylose glue. Use cachous, blossoms, love hearts, butterflies or even spots to decorate aprons.

STAGE TWO

4. *Assembling.* Attach each head to its body by inserting a candy stick through side of the cupcake papers. You may need to use the point of a knife to cut through paper so stick can be inserted easily.

cakestar 110

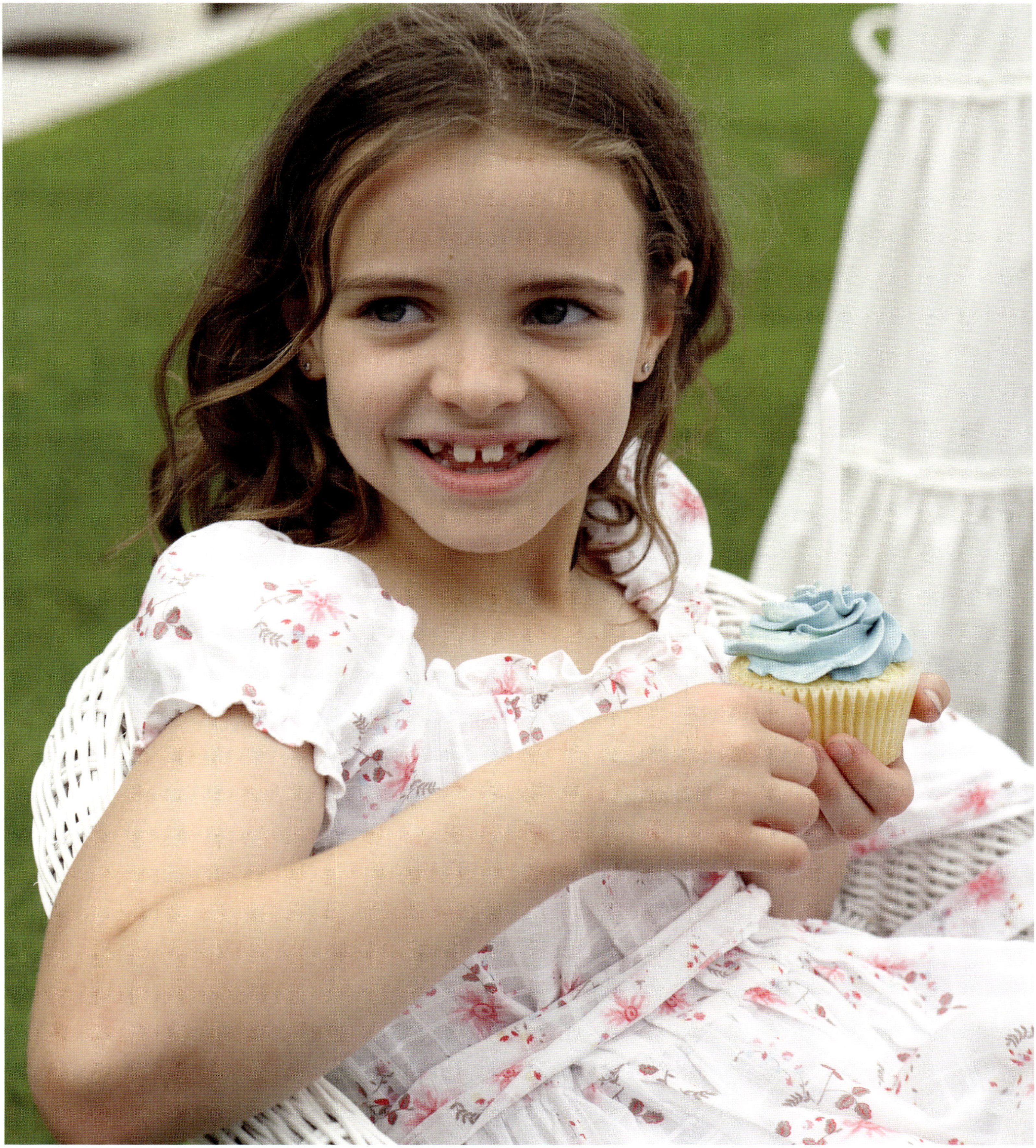

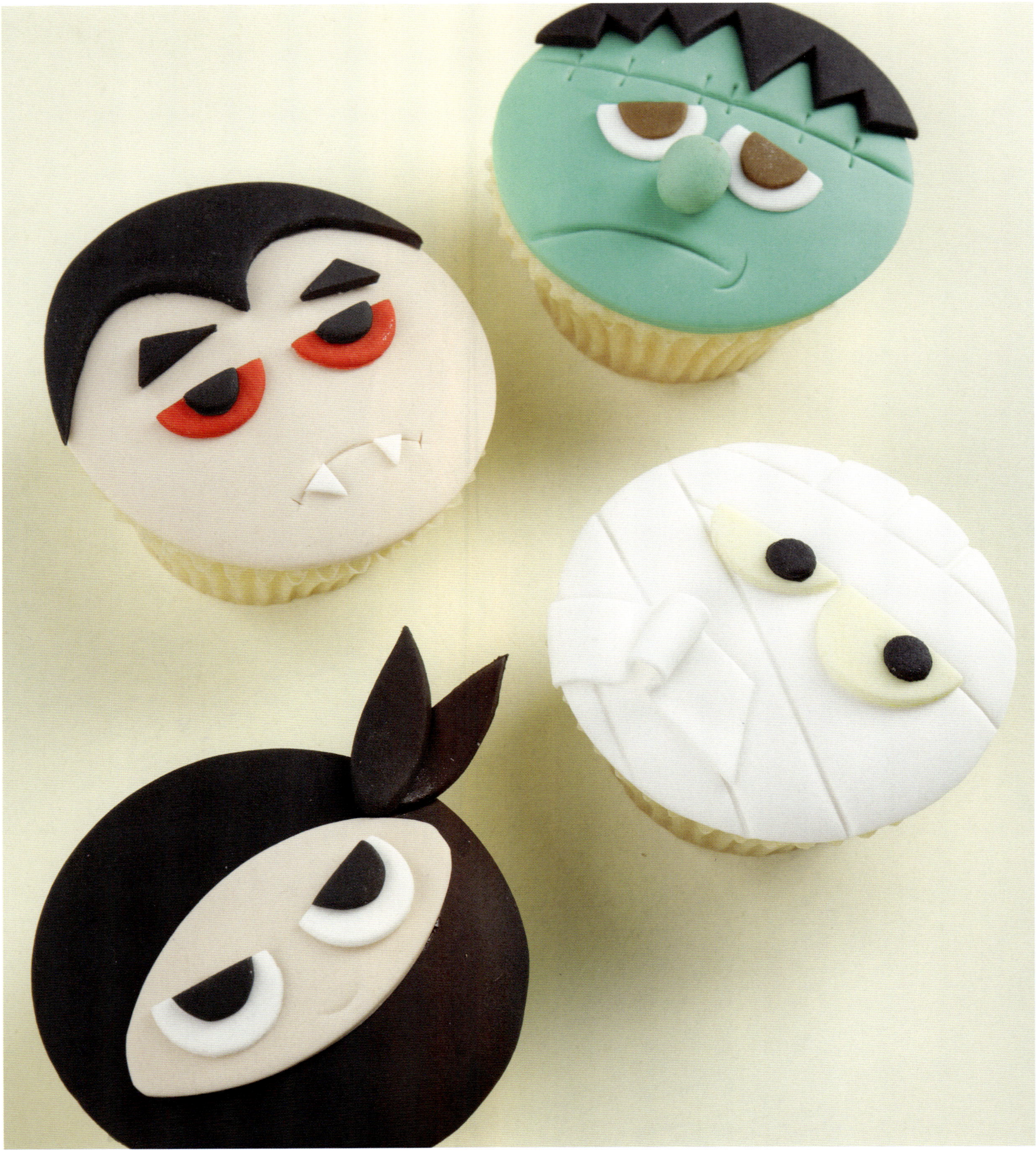

not so cute cupcakes

With four fun ways to decorate cupcakes, you can invite these scary friends along to your next party. Or create armies of ninjas clad in black and white for a good versus evil battle, or even make lolly-pink girl ninjas. Makes 24.

CAKE REQUIREMENTS

- 24 medium cupcakes (see pages 16–17)

DECORATING INGREDIENTS

- ½ x buttercream recipe (see page 13)
- 1.52 kg fondant icing (pre-coloured store-bought or coloured with gel paste food colouring), set aside in plastic wrap
    - 450 g black
    - 360 g skin colour (made using pink, brown and yellow pastes)
    - 350 g white
    - 20 g pale yellow
    - 300 g green
    - 20 g brown
    - 20 g red
- pure icing sugar (for kneading)
- cornflour (for rolling out)
- tylose powder
- tylose glue (see page 15)

EQUIPMENT

- templates (see page 136)
- small palette knife
- fine sieve (for sifting icing sugar when kneading)
- small rolling pin
- smoother
- knife
- circle cutters and round piping tips
- small paintbrush (for applying tylose glue)
- cocktail sticks

cakestar 114

cupcake Ninja

Makes 6

STAGE ONE

1. *Icing cupcakes.* Coat 6 cupcakes in buttercream icing then fondant-ice in black (see page 21).

STAGE TWO

2. *Face.* Roll out skin-coloured fondant to 3 mm thick. Using knife and face template, cut out shapes for faces and indent noses with edge of a small circle cutter or piping tip. Stick in place on each cupcake with tylose glue.
3. *Eyes.* Cut 2 white rounds for each face using a 1.75-cm circle cutter and 2 black rounds using a 1-cm circle cutter or round piping tip. Stick black rounds on top of white rounds then trim to size with knife, cutting just above centre. Use tylose glue to position eyes on faces.
4. *Ties.* Knead tylose powder (see page 15) into black fondant, roll out to 3 mm thick and cut 2 teardrop shapes for ties using side of a small circle cutter. Stick these just above the face with pointed ends slightly off edge of cupcake. Support with a cocktail stick until dry.

Yummy Mummy

Makes 6

STAGE ONE

1. *Icing cupcakes.* Coat 6 cupcakes in buttercream icing then fondant-ice in white (see page 21).

STAGE TWO

2. *Bandages.* While fondant is still soft, use back of a knife to indent bandage pattern. Roll out a piece of white fondant to 2 mm thick and cut a thin rectangle for each cupcake. Stick in place as an unravelling bandage.
3. *Eyes.* Roll out pale yellow fondant to 3 mm thick. Using a 2.5-cm circle cutter, cut out a round for each mummy. Cut round at an uneven angle and stick in place as eyes. Add 2 black rounds for pupils, cut using the end of a piping tip.

cakestar 116

count cupcake

Makes 6

STAGE ONE

1. *Icing cupcakes.* Coat 6 cupcakes in buttercream icing then fondant-ice in skin colour (see page 21).

STAGE TWO

2. *Face.* While fondant is still soft, use a circle cutter to indent mouth, making a small line at each end with the point of a knife.
3. *Hair.* Roll out black fondant to 3 mm thick. Using same circle cutter used for skin colour, cut out a round of black fondant and use a smaller circle cutter to cut out curved sections. Use a knife to cut out small black triangles for eyebrows.
4. *Eyes.* Roll out red icing to 3 mm thick. Using 2-cm circle cutter, cut a round for each count. Cut round in half and stick in place as eyes. Cut a black round using the end of a piping tip, cut this in half and stick in position using tylose glue.
5. *Teeth.* Roll out a piece of white fondant to 2 mm thick and cut small triangles for teeth. Stick in place with tylose glue.

frankentreat

Makes 6

STAGE ONE

1. *Icing cupcakes.* Coat 6 cupcakes in buttercream icing then fondant-ice in green (see page 21).

STAGE TWO

2. *Scar and mouth.* While fondant is still soft, use knife to indent stitching pattern and circle cutter to mark the mouth.
3. *Hair.* Roll out black fondant to 3 mm thick. Using same circle cutter used for face, cut out a round of black fondant for each and use knife to cut jagged hair then stick in place using tylose glue.
4. *Eyes.* Roll out white icing to 3 mm thick. Using 1.75-cm circle cutter, cut 2 rounds for each monster, then cut smaller brown rounds and glue in position. Use knife to trim top from each pair of circles to achieve correct shape. Position eyes on cupcakes.
5. *Nose.* Roll a pea-sized ball of green fondant and stick in place.

3 6 6

dressed to impress

These cupcakes mean business. Even the most fashion-tragic of ties becomes tasteful when made from sugar on yummy cupcakes. Makes 12.

CAKE REQUIREMENTS

- 12 large cupcakes (see pages 16–17)

DECORATING INGREDIENTS

- ½ x buttercream recipe (see page 13)
- 1.1 kg fondant icing (pre-coloured store-bought or coloured with gel paste food colouring), set aside in plastic wrap
    - 250 g white
    - 250 g pink
    - 250 g blue
    - 100 g skin colour (made using pink, brown and yellow colours)
    - 250 g total of various colours
- pure icing sugar (for kneading)
- cornflour (for rolling out)
- tylose glue (see page 15)

EQUIPMENT

- small palette knife
- fine sieve (for sifting icing sugar when kneading)
- small rolling pin
- circle cutters
- knife
- small paintbrush (for applying tylose glue)
- ruler
- templates (see page 137)

STAGE ONE

1. *Icing cupcakes.* Coat cupcakes in buttercream icing and then fondant-ice in each shirt colour (see page 21). There is enough fondant allowed to make 4 shirts each in white, blue and pink.

STAGE TWO

2. *Shirt front.* While fondant is still soft, use knife to indent a line down the centre of each cupcake.
3. *Neck.* Roll out skin-coloured icing to 3 mm thick, use knife to cut around neck template and stick in place on each cupcake.
4. *Ties.* To create tie-died effect, roll lengths of each of your selected tie colours together into a larger snake of icing, folding and rolling again, before rolling out with rolling pin to 3 mm thick. Use tie template and knife to cut to size. It is best to cut all ties from icing at once, if possible, as the colours tend to over-blend when re-rolled. Stick in position using tylose glue and use the tip of the knife to mark knot in tie.
5. *Collars.* Roll out icing 3 mm thick to match each shirt colour, using ruler and knife to trim into 9-cm long strips that are 7 mm wide. Use paintbrush to apply tylose glue around edges of triangular neck piece. Gently press on back of each collar, folding sides inwards to create rest of collar and trim to length.
6. *Pockets.* Roll out icing 3 mm thick to match each shirt colour, then use knife to cut 1.5-cm squares, trimming bottom 2 corners from these. Glue into position and use knife to mark a seam across top of each pocket.

Dinner Shirt: By marking extra lines down your iced cupcake, replacing tie with bow tie and adding some tiny buttons cut with a piping tip, you can take these cupcakes from boardroom to ballroom.

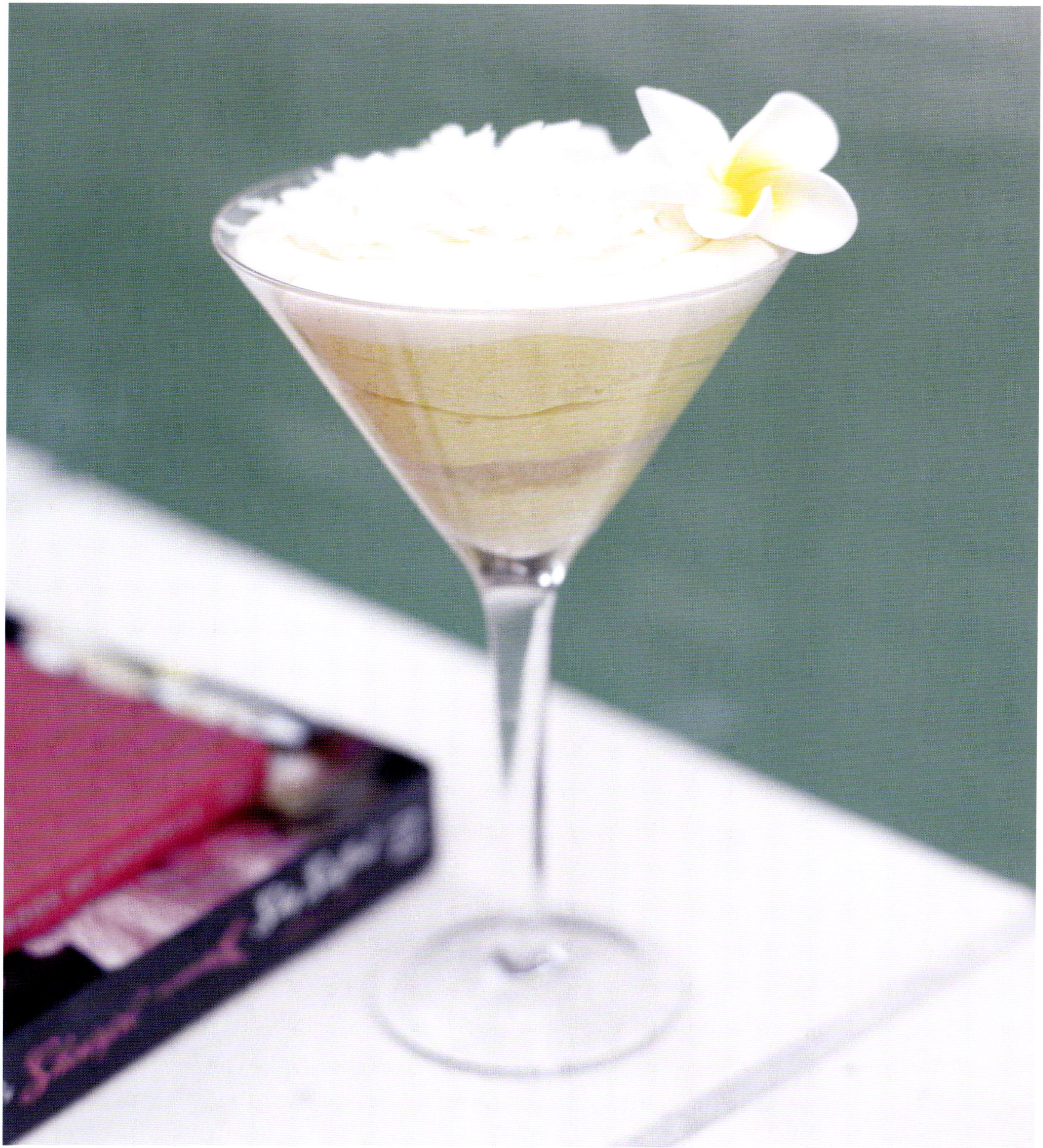

cupcake colada

Sassy women who indulge in cocktails and cupcakes, raise your glasses because here's how you can have your cocktail and eat your cake, too! Best served while wearing Manolo Blahniks. Makes 6.

CAKE REQUIREMENTS

- 6 large cupcakes (see pages 16–17)
- 6 medium cupcakes (see pages 16–17)

DECORATING INGREDIENTS

- cornflour (for rolling out and to support drying flowers)
- ½ x flower paste recipe (see recipe opposite), stored in plastic wrap
- pure icing sugar (for kneading if flower paste too soft)
- tylose glue (see page 15)
- yellow petal dust
- ⅓ cup crushed pineapple, well drained
- 1½ x buttercream recipe (see page 13)
- yellow food colouring
- ½ cup coconut rum (such as Malibu)
- ½ x sugar syrup recipe (see recipe page 123)
- fresh flaked coconut

EQUIPMENT

- 6 martini glasses
- small palette knife
- fine sieve (for sifting icing sugar when kneading)
- small rolling pin
- knife
- frangipani cutter
- petal pad
- medium ball tool
- soft paintbrush
- small paintbrush (for applying tylose glue)
- 2 large piping bags
- 2 couplers
- 2 large round piping tips (1 cm diameter)
- container (for drying flowers)

FLOWER PASTE

450 g pure icing sugar, sifted
4 level tsp gelatine
¼ cup water
2 heaped tsp glucose syrup

Sift icing sugar into bowl. Place gelatine and water into separate small heatproof bowl. Stand bowl in a saucepan containing a little water and dissolve gelatine over gentle heat. When liquid is clear and gelatine fully dissolved, add glucose. Make a well in centre of icing sugar and stir in liquid with a knife to form a paste. Place paste in an airtight bag in an airtight container, and store at room temperature for at least 3 hours before using. If paste is too sticky to work with, knead in a little more sifted icing sugar.

1

2

3

3

6

10

10

10

cakestar 122

STAGE ONE

1. *Making frangipani flowers.* Shaping petals. Make one flower at a time to avoid drying and cracking. On a surface dusted with cornflour, roll out flower paste to a very thin, even thickness and cut 5 petals. Place petals on a petal pad and use a medium ball tool to cup left side of each petal by pressing at the top and gently pulling back towards the point.
2. *Joining petals.* To form flower, apply tylose glue to left side of each petal from the point, extending a third of the way up the petal. Arrange petals in a fan shape so they slightly overlap and press to secure. Roll up 'fan' so the first petal curls just inside the last petal and pinch at base to close.
3. *Opening flower.* Use ball tool to make a small indent in a container of cornflour, sit closed frangipani in this and carefully open the petals out using your fingers or a soft paintbrush.
4. Repeat for remaining 5 flowers.
5. Allow to dry for at least 24 hours.
6. *Colouring.* Once flowers have dried, remove from cornflour and brush off excess cornflour with a soft paintbrush. Dust centres with yellow petal dust.

STAGE TWO

7. *Preparing pineapple buttercream.* For a smooth texture, blitz drained pineapple in short bursts in a food processor. It does not have to be completely puréed, but reducing lumps makes it far easier to pipe with. Too much liquid will cause buttercream to split or curdle. Place half prepared buttercream in a bowl and beat in pineapple. Add yellow food colouring a drop at a time until a pale yellow colour is reached.
8. *Preparing coconut buttercream.* To remaining buttercream add ¼ cup coconut rum. Beat well to combine.

STAGE THREE

9. *Preparing cupcakes.* Combine remaining ¼ cup of coconut rum with sugar syrup. Cut all cupcakes in half and brush generously with flavoured syrup to moisten.
10. *Filling glasses.* Place pineapple buttercream in a piping bag fitted with a large round piping tip. Pipe a small amount of pineapple buttercream into the bottom of each glass and press base of a medium cupcake on top. Pipe another thin layer of pineapple buttercream on this, press top of the cupcake on top, then repeat with more pineapple buttercream and large cupcake halves. The number of layers you fit in may vary, depending on the depth of the glasses you use. Finish with a cupcake layer on top.
11. *Coconut topping.* With coconut rum buttercream in a separate piping bag fitted with a large round piping tip, pipe a neat swirl of icing to cover the top cupcake, filling to the edge of the glass.
12. *Finishing touches.* Sprinkle with fresh flaked coconut. Place flowers on up to an hour before serving.

SUGAR SYRUP

½ cup water
½ cup sugar

Combine ingredients in a small saucepan over medium heat and stir until sugar is dissolved. Allow to boil briefly and then reduce heat and simmer for 5 minutes. Allow the sugar syrup to return to room temperature before flavouring or using.

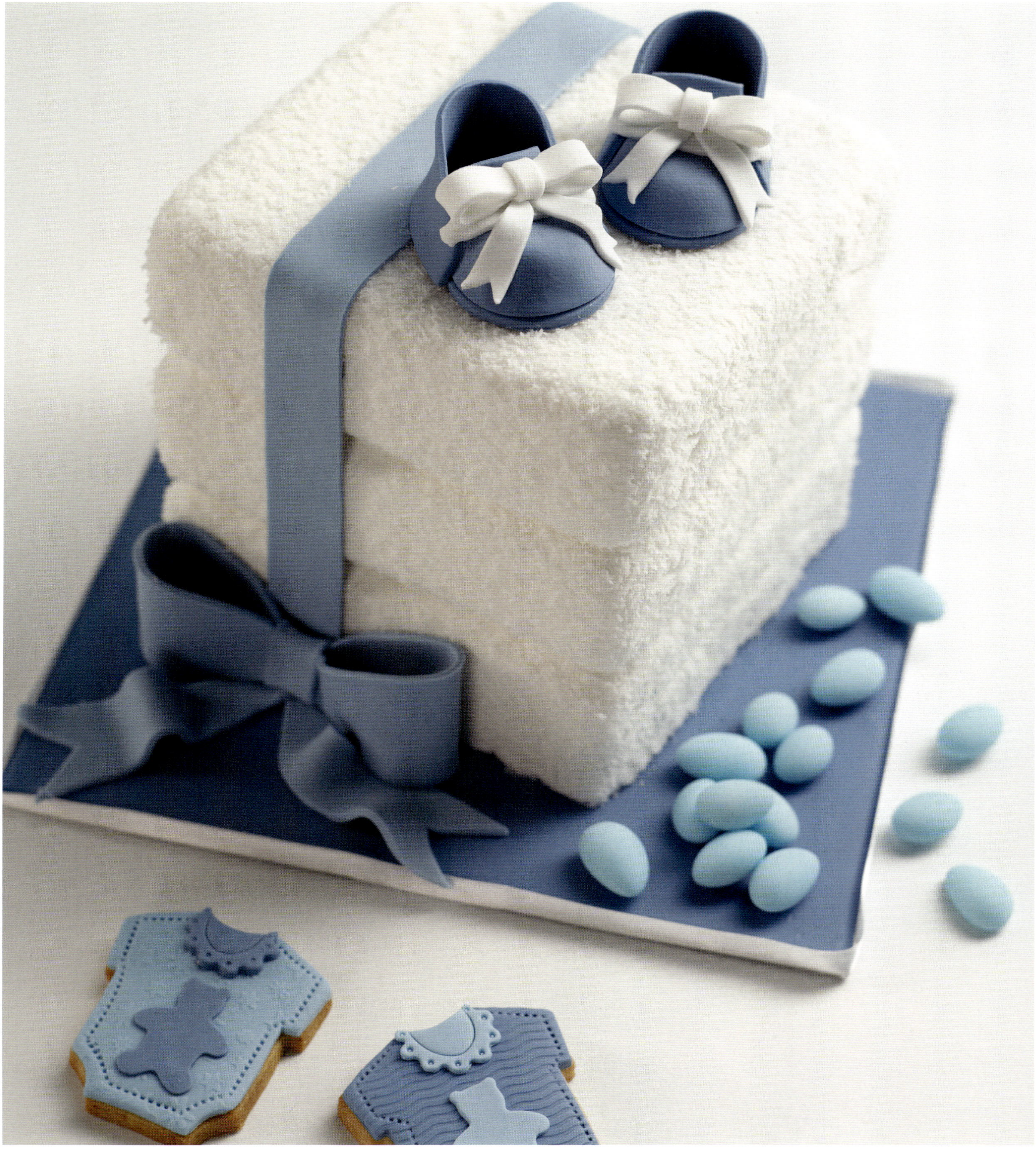

welcome bundle

Prepare for the joy of a new arrival with these fluffy nappies stacked high and topped with tiny sugar booties.

CAKE REQUIREMENTS
- 2 x 15-cm (6") square cakes

DECORATING INGREDIENTS
- 1 x ganache recipe (see page 13)
- 1 x apricot glaze recipe (see page 15)
- ½ x royal icing recipe (see page 14)
- 1 egg white
- 1 cup desiccated coconut
- 2.25 kg fondant icing (pre-coloured store-bought or coloured with gel paste food colouring), set aside in plastic wrap
    - 400 g medium blue
    - 1.6 kg white
    - 250 g pale blue
- pure icing sugar (for kneading)
- cornflour (for rolling out)
- tylose powder
- tylose glue (see page 15)

EQUIPMENT
- 25-cm (10") square heavy cake board
- 1.2 m white ribbon (10–15 mm wide)
- templates (see page 140)
- serrated knife
- large palette knife
- straight-edged scraper
- pastry brush
- fine sieve (for sifting icing sugar when kneading)
- large and small rolling pins
- knife
- craft knife
- smoothers
- small paintbrush (for applying tylose glue)
- number 2 piping tip
- coupler and piping bag
- non-stick baking paper (for under cake and drying decorations)
- cotton balls (for shaping and drying booties)
- teaspoon
- Dresden tool
- ruler
- scissors
- non-toxic glue

Add to the fun by creating cute 'onesie' cookies – let your decorating skills run wild.

cakestar 125

cakestar 126

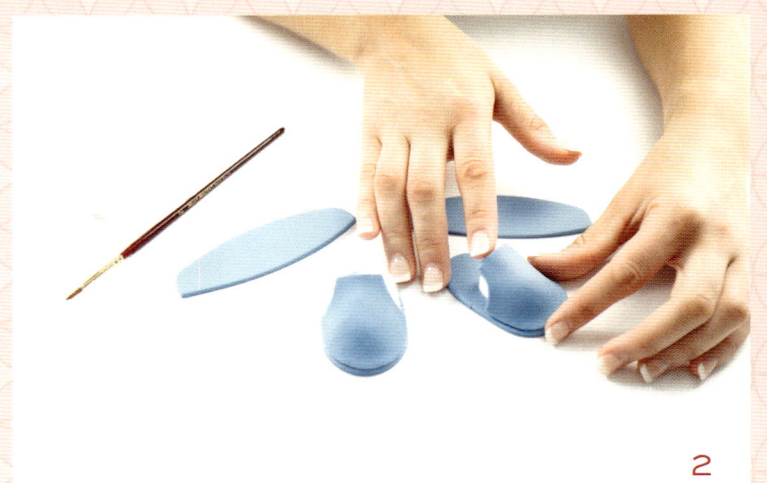

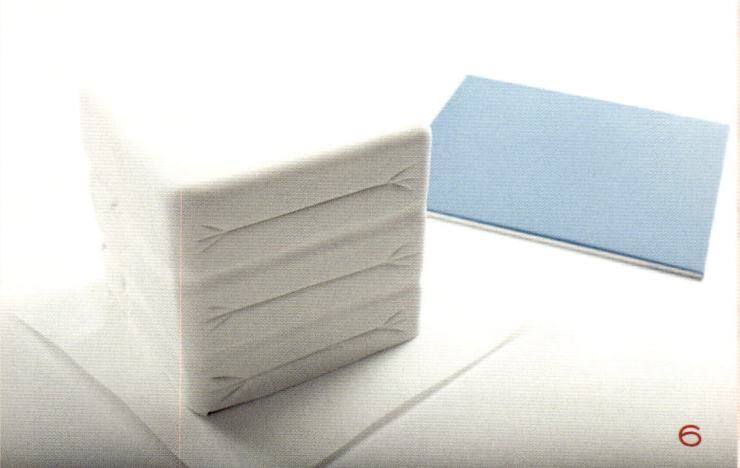

STAGE ONE

1. *Forming the booties.* Knead tylose powder (see page 15) into medium blue fondant and roll out to 3 mm thick. Use knife or craft knife to cut out 2 pieces with each of the templates to make 2 booties.
2. Working quickly so fondant doesn't dry and crack, apply tylose glue to toe of each sole, then place tops of the booties in position, placing a cotton ball inside each to help shape them and as support while icing dries.
3. Put tylose glue where backs of the booties will attach and press in place.
4. *Bows.* Knead tylose powder into 50 g of white fondant and roll out to 3 mm thick. Cut a strip 1 cm wide and 5 cm long for each bootie. Glue one across the top of each, as pictured, pinching ends where they meet the sides. For the tails of each bow, cut 2 strips 1 cm wide and 3 cm long and cut a V into one end of each. Glue in place, then form the loop of each bow with a strip of fondant 1 cm wide by 10 cm long. Cover joins with another short strip. Glue in place with tylose glue.
5. Set aside completed booties to dry on non-stick baking paper. Once dry, remove cotton balls.

STAGE TWO

6. *Prepare cakes.* Level cakes by removing crust from top of each to give a flat surface. Sandwich one on top of other using ganache. To create illusion of 3 separate nappies piled high, use serrated knife to cut 2 small, evenly spaced grooves all around the cake. Lift cake onto a sheet of non-stick baking paper and cover with ganache (see page 19), then use a teaspoon to define grooves in ganache.
7. Allow cake to set overnight, if possible.

The booties can be made well before the cake is decorated. This is not completely necessary, but allows plenty of drying time and helps with time management.

cakestar 128

STAGE THREE

8. *Cover cake.* Brush cake with apricot glaze and cover with kneaded white fondant (see page 19). Smooth and trim off any excess fondant.
9. *Mark the folded nappies.* While fondant on cake is still soft, use the side of your hand to press fondant into grooves previously cut in cake, then mark fold lines on 2 opposing sides with Dresden tool.
10. *Cover board.* Brush board with tylose glue. Knead remaining medium blue fondant and roll out a little larger than board. Place fondant on board, and smooth and trim edges. Trim edge of cake board with ribbon, using non-toxic glue to fasten.
11. *Texture.* Use 1 tablespoon of egg white to dilute ¼ cup of royal icing to a consistency that can be brushed onto cake with a pastry brush. Cover entire cake in an even coating and immediately press desiccated coconut on top of this. Use Dresden tool to re-mark fold lines so they are clearly visible.
12. *Position cake.* Pipe royal icing onto centre of board. Carefully remove cake from baking paper and lift onto the board, pressing down with a smoother to ensure it is securely in place.

STAGE FOUR

13. *Position booties.* Use a small dot of royal icing underneath each of the booties to secure in place.
14. *Ribbon.* Roll out pale blue fondant to 3 mm thick and use ruler and knife to cut strip 4 cm wide by 55 cm long. Use royal icing to stick in place and trim to length with a knife.
15. *Bow.* Use template on page 138 as a guide to cut out the pieces for bow. Firstly attach tailpieces to where ribbon meets cake board. Fold long piece into a loop and attach ends using tylose glue, then glue knot in place. Attach bow to cake and tailpieces using tylose glue.

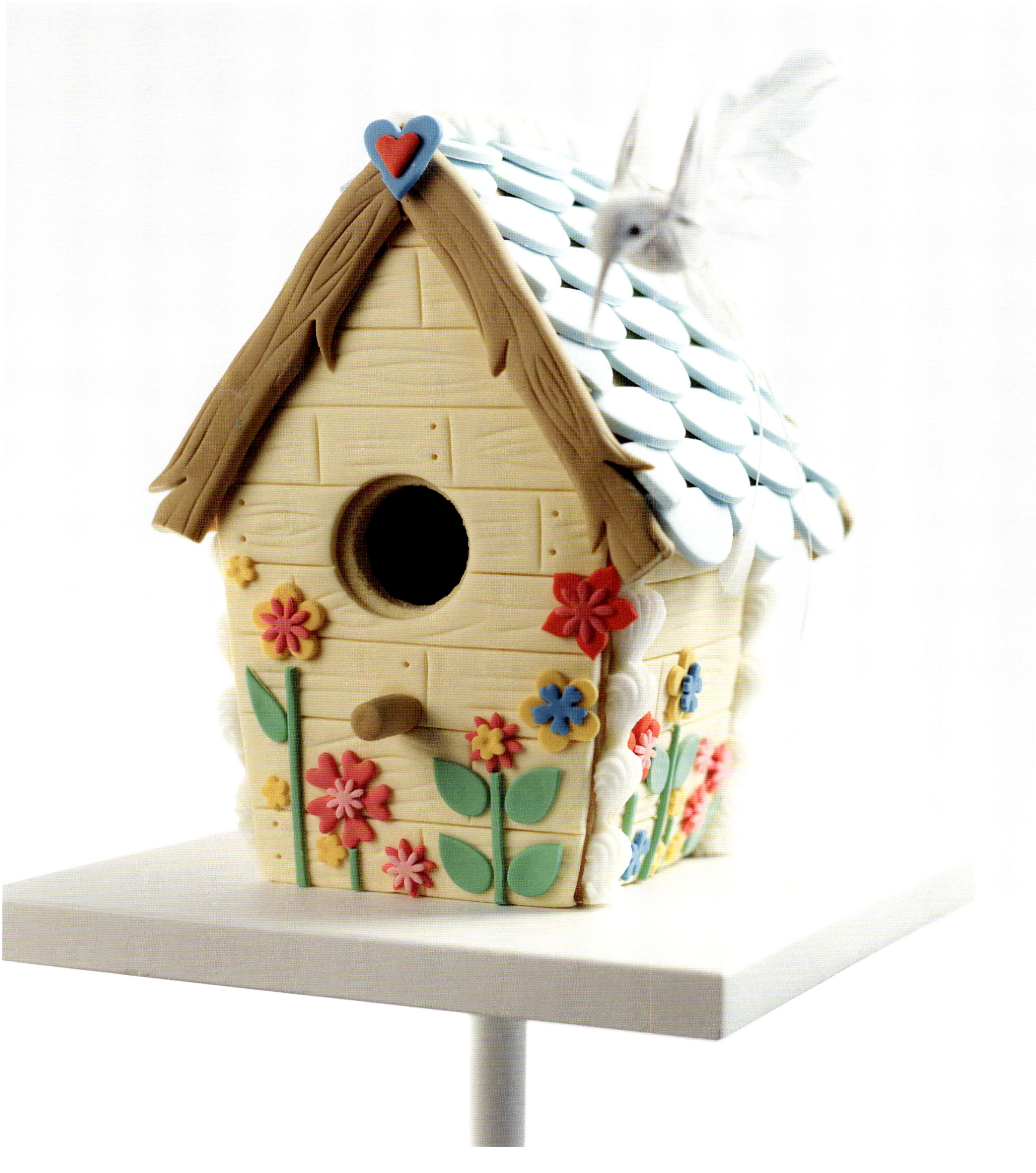

vanilla bean birdhouse

I always think of the house made from confectionery in the tale of Hansel and Gretel when I make these sugary sweet birdhouses. Fill your birdhouse with beautifully wrapped treats, such as chocolates and trinkets, before you put the roof in place.

CAKE REQUIREMENTS

- 2 x Vanilla Bean Biscuit recipe in shapes of the templates (see page 18). Use any leftover dough to make little bird biscuits.

DECORATING INGREDIENTS

- 2 x royal icing recipe (see page 14)
- 1.55 kg fondant icing (pre-coloured store-bought or coloured with gel paste food colouring), set aside in plastic wrap
    - 850 g pale yellow
    - 300 g pale blue
    - 120 g brown
    - 15 g bright blue
    - 15 g red
    - 50 g green
    - 200 g total of various colours for flowers
- pure icing sugar (for kneading)
- cornflour (for rolling out)
- tylose powder
- tylose glue (see page 15)
- 1 piece dried spaghetti

EQUIPMENT

- 23-cm (9") square cake board
- fine sieve (for sifting icing sugar when kneading)
- large and small rolling pins
- smoother
- circle cutters
- knife
- small paintbrush (for applying tylose glue)
- cocktail sticks
- ruler
- Dresden tool
- flower or blossom cutters
- leaf cutter
- small and medium heart cutters
- large star piping tip
- number 2 piping tip
- coupler and piping bag
- 2 drinking glasses to support drying structure
- dressmaker's pin

To save time, you can use store-bought sugar flowers to decorate your birdhouse and the roof can be covered in a single piece of fondant.

cakestar 132

STAGE ONE

1. *Icing walls.* With same template used to cut biscuit shapes, cut icing shapes to decorate walls from pale yellow fondant that has been rolled out to 3 mm thick. Stick in place using royal icing and smooth (see page 22). While icing is still soft, line up all walls and use ruler to mark timber planks. Use Dresden tool to add wood-like texture. Mark tiny holes with cocktail stick to look like nail holes.
2. *Icing roof.* Roll out pale blue fondant to 3 mm thick. Cut rounds using 5-cm circle cutter then cut these in half to create little shingles. Use royal icing to glue in place, beginning at what will be the bottom of each roof and working your way up. Overlap each layer slightly and trim any overhanging pieces to give a neat edge.
3. Allow wall and roof panels to dry for a short while before assembly. This will ensure everything is secure before it is stood up and will reduce the risk of you marking the fondant when handling.

STAGE TWO

4. *Assembling walls.* Use 2 drinking glasses placed in the centre of cake board to support walls while you position them. With a piping bag fitted with a large star tip, pipe a line of icing along the base of each wall panel as you secure it in place.
5. *Concealing wall joins.* Check that roof panels are going to fit and, once you are happy with positioning of walls, use same piping tip to do a scalloped or shell border that will conceal and strengthen the joins. This is achieved by joining a series of teardrop-shaped piping together (see page 23).
6. Allow royal icing to set completely before removing glasses, adding any wrapped treats and putting the roof in position. Setting may take several hours but is essential to avoid structure collapsing.

STAGE THREE

7. *Positioning roof.* Pipe a line of royal icing along tops of each wall where they will join the roof. Position roof, supporting with the drinking glasses if needed. Use same shell border technique to cover join along roof peak.

You will find an array of bird-inspired stationery and party décor online – this is a fabulous theme for christenings, first birthdays, baby showers and garden parties.

cakestar 134

STAGE FOUR

8. *Roof trim.* Knead tylose powder (see page 15) into brown fondant and roll into 4 x 15-cm-long sausages. Flatten with small rolling pin and use knife and Dresden tool to give a wood-like finish. Trim and stick in place along front and back of birdhouse roof. Conceal join at the top with hearts cut from thinly rolled bright blue and red fondant. Roll offcuts of brown fondant into a 3-cm-long sausage, insert a piece of dried spaghetti for support and attach as perch below opening at front using royal icing to stick in place. Support perch by inserting a dressmaker's pin underneath until it dries in place.

9. *Flowers.* Use various small blossom cutters to cut flower shapes from thinly rolled coloured fondant. Stems are cut from green fondant using ruler and knife. Cut leaves from same green fondant with small leaf cutter (or petal cutter). Use tylose glue to attach these around the sides of your birdhouse.

10. *Storage.* If you are not going to serve the birdhouse on the day it is completed, wrap carefully in cellophane to keep the biscuits from going soft.

11. *Love heart birds.* These sweet singing birds are the perfect inhabitants for your Vanilla Bean Birdhouse. Bake and decorate using template on page 137, a heart cutter as the wing and tiny triangle for the beak. You should have more than adequate fondant remaining from decorating your birdhouse; these birds make perfect use of offcuts. Eyes are piped with black royal icing or can be marked with a black food-colouring pen. For the most beautiful presentation, cut a hole in the dough with a piping tip before baking and thread the decorated biscuits onto fine ribbon. Paint branches with white non-toxic spray paint, arrange in vases and hang your birds as table centrepieces.

templates

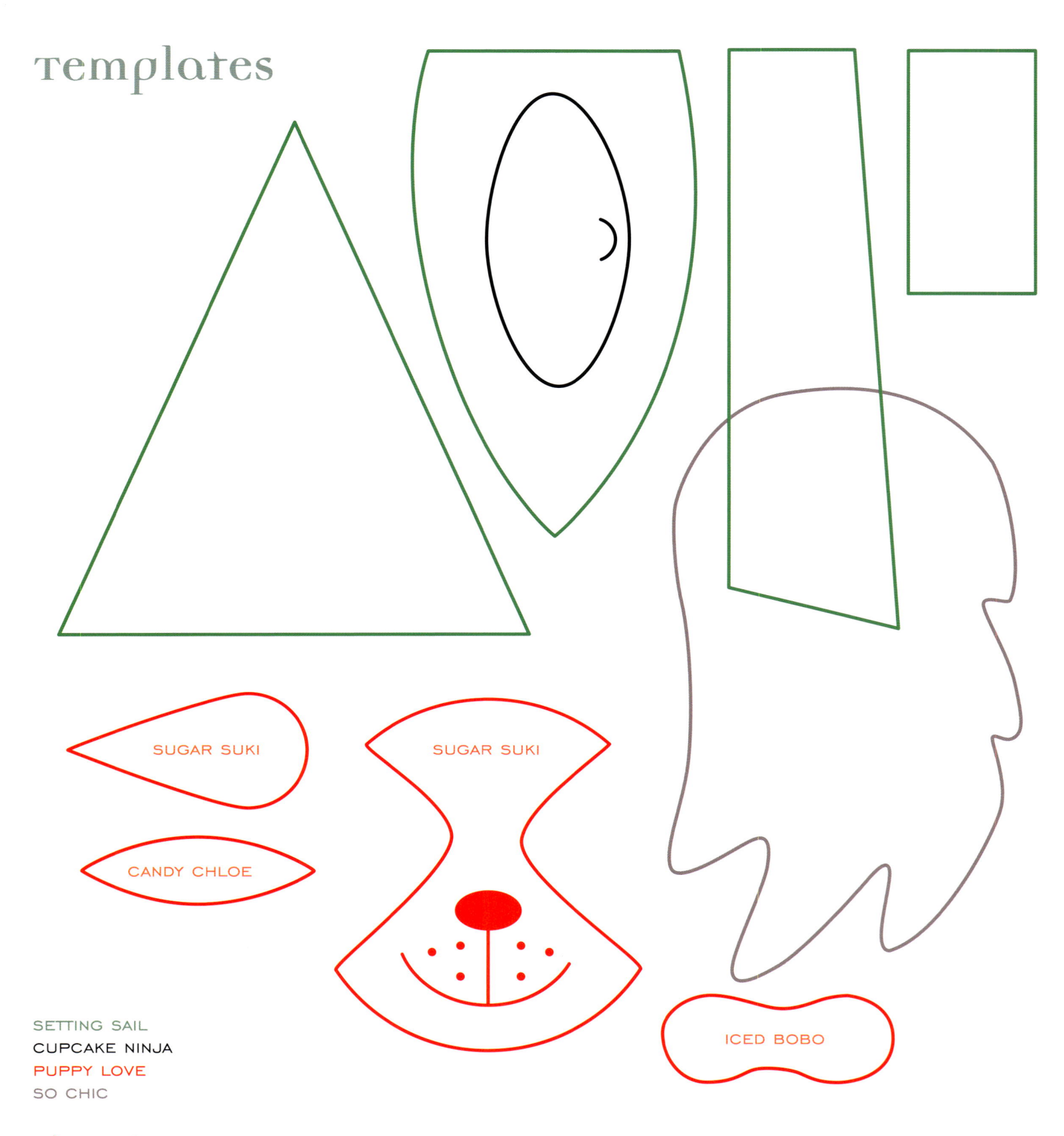

SUGAR SUKI

SUGAR SUKI

CANDY CHLOE

ICED BOBO

SETTING SAIL
CUPCAKE NINJA
PUPPY LOVE
SO CHIC

cakestar 136

TUXEDOS AND TIARAS
LOVE HEART BIRDS
DRESSED TO IMPRESS
CAKE FAIRY
IT'S A GOAL
WE'LL ALWAYS HAVE PARIS

cakestar 137

MUSICAL SILHOUETTE
LACED UP / WELCOME BUNDLE

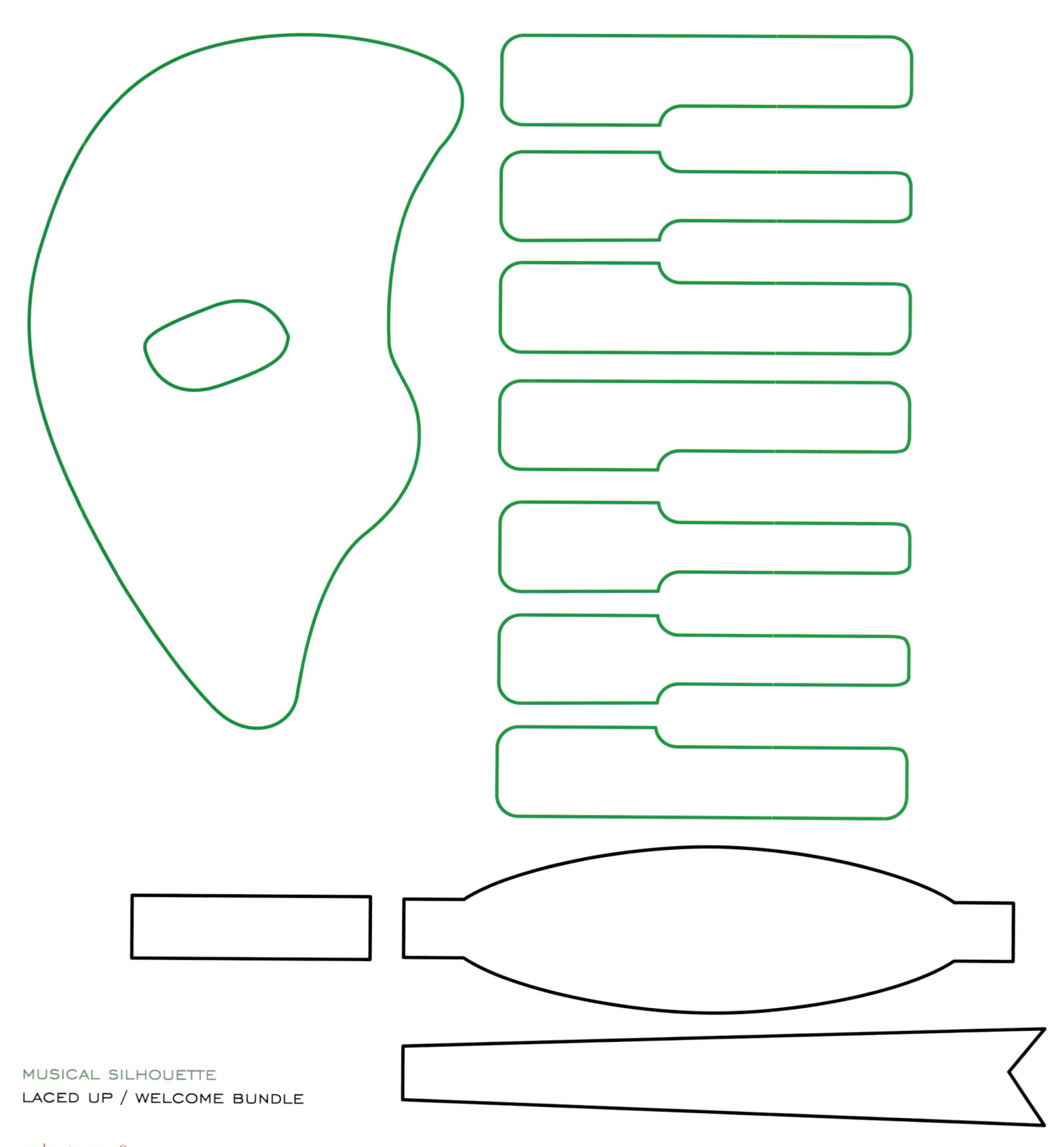

cakestar 138

BUZZING BEE
IN FULL BLOOM

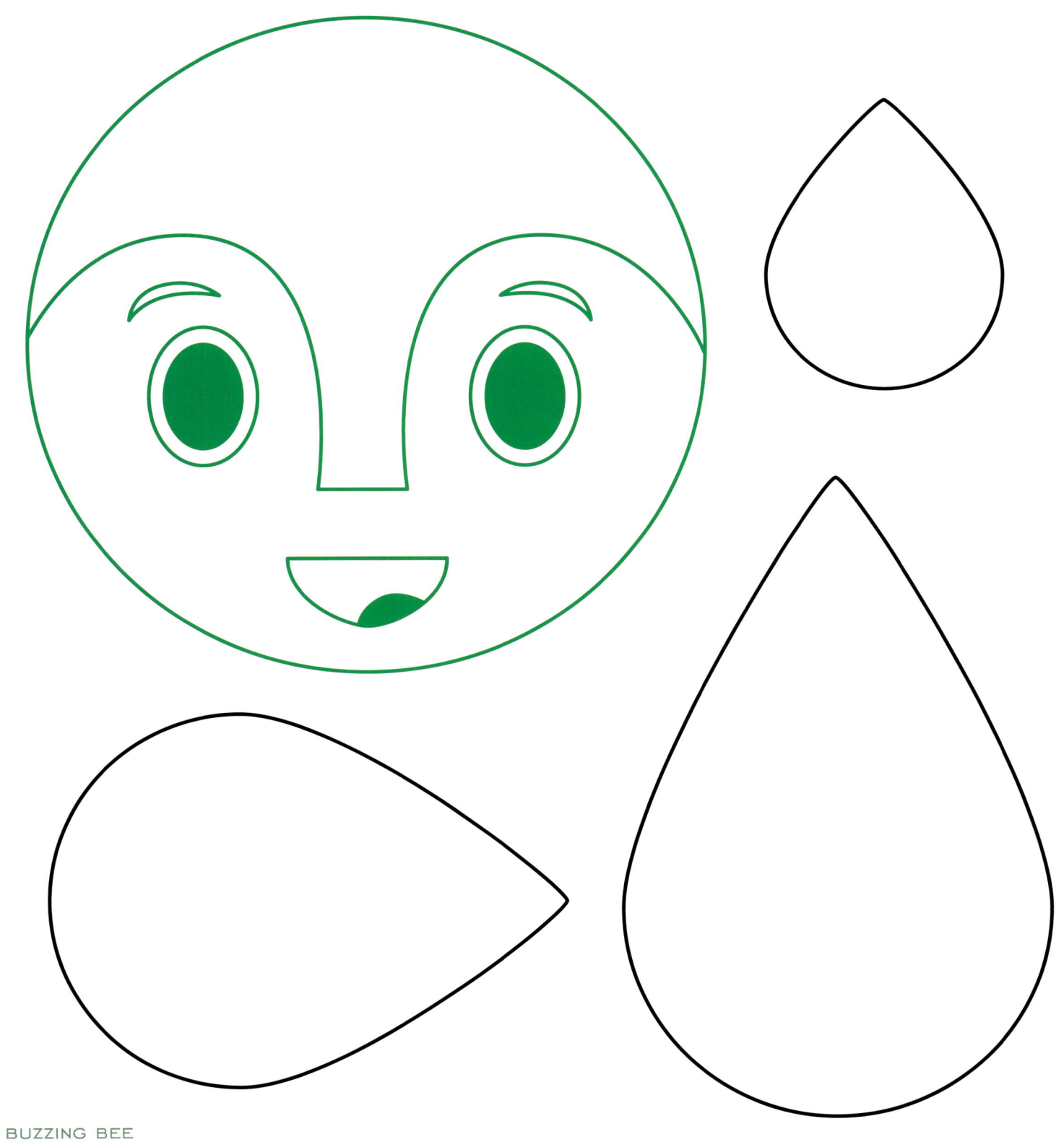

cakestar 139

HERO TIME (1 OF 2)
WELCOME BUNDLE

cakestar 140

HERO TIME (2 OF 2)
PERFECT FIT

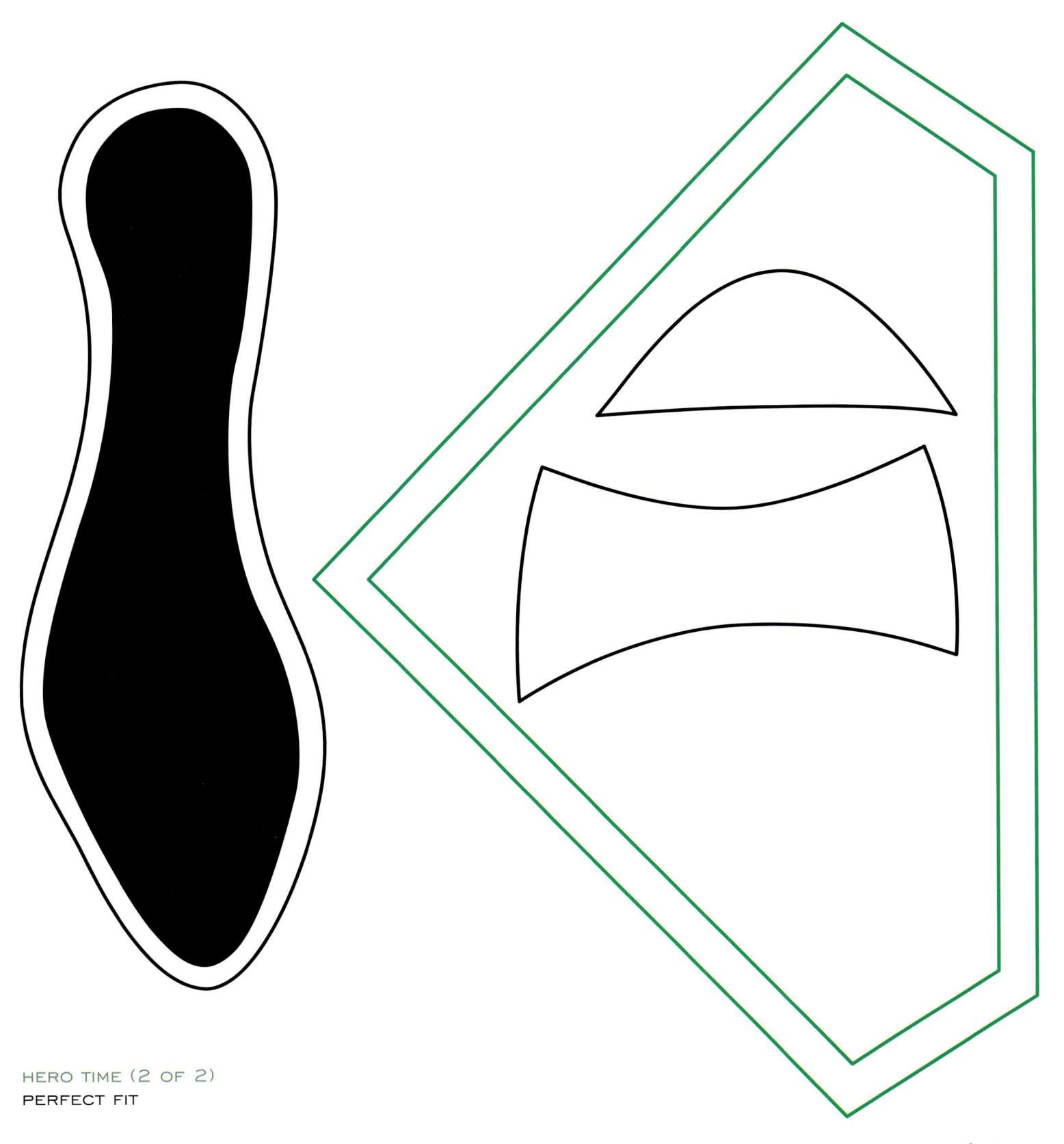

index

A
alcohol content in cakes 17
apricot glaze 15

B
ball-shaped and rounded tins 17
ball tool 8, 9
Bakels Pettinice RTR Icing 14
biscuit designs
    Love Heart Birds 134–5, 137 (t)
    Vanilla Bean Birdhouse 130–5
    Wonderful Time, A 66–9
biscuits 18, 22
    flavouring 18
    fondant icing 22
    storage 18
    vanilla bean biscuits 18
buttercream 13
    icing on cupcakes 21, *21*
Buzzing Bee 44–7, 139 (t)

C
cachous 10, 11
cake boards 8, 9
    covering with fondant 21
cake-decorating supplies 10–11
cake designs
    Buzzing Bee 44–7, 139 (t)
    Cake Fairy 84–9, 137 (t)
    Hero Time 30–3, 140–1 (t)
    In Full Bloom 34–9, 139 (t)
    It's a Goal 70–3, 137 (t)
    Laced Up 48–51, 138 (t)
    Musical Silhouette 34–5, 138 (t)
    Perfect Fit 56–9, 141 (t)
    Setting Sail 74–7, 136 (t)
    So Chic 52–5
    Sweets for the Sweet 78–82
    Teatale Party 60–4
    Tuxedos and Tiaras 26–9, 137 (t)
    Welcome Bundle 124–9, 140 (t)
Cake Fairy 84–9, 137 (t)
cakes
    alcohol content in 17
    ball-shaped 17
    basic recipes for 16–17
    covering with ganache 19
    double chocolate cake 17
    flavouring 16
    layering technique 19
    levelling technique 19
    preparing tin 17
    white chocolate & vanilla cake 16
Candy Chloe 106–7, 136 (t)
caramel flavouring 16
cases, cupcakes 8, 9, 17
chocolate curls 10, 11
chocolate ganache, dark 13
chocolate hearts 10, 11
citrus flavouring 16
CMC (carboxymethyl cellulose) gum 15
colouring icing 22–3
cornflour 20
Count Cupcake 116–17
Cupcake Aquariums 100–3
Cupcake Colada 120–23
cupcake designs
    Cupcake Aquariums 100–3
    Cupcake Colada 120–23
    Cute as a Button Bouquet 90–5
    Dressed to Impress 118–19, 137 (t)
    Not So Cute Cupcakes 112–17
    Oh! Babushka 108–11
    Petit Tiered Cakes 40–3
    Puppy Love 104–7, 136 (t)
    We'll Always Have Paris 96–9, 137 (t)
Cupcake Ninja 114–15, 136 (t)
cupcakes
    alcohol content in 17
    basic recipes for 16–17
    cases 8, 9, 17
    double chocolate 17
    flavouring 16
    icing techniques 21
    levelling 21
    preparing trays 17
    storing tips 7
    white chocolate & vanilla 16
Cute as a Button Bouquet 90–5
cutters, metal and plastic 8, 9

D
dark chocolate ganache 13
decorations, edible 10–11, 23
    drying 23
decorator's alcohol 23
decorator's glue *see* tylose glue
Dolly Varden cake tin 85
dragées *see* cachous
Dresden tool 8, 9
Dressed to Impress 118–19, 137 (t)

E
edible decorations 10–11
edible glue 15
edible lustres 10, 11, 23
eggs, tips for using 14
equipment for decoration 8–9

F
foam pad 8, 9
fondant icing 14–15, 21–3
    biscuits (technique) 22
    cake boards (technique) 21
    cakes (technique) 20
    colouring (technique) 22
    cupcakes (technique) 21
    quick modelling 14–15
    storage 14
food-colouring pen 8, 9
food colours, paste and liquid 10, 11, 22–3
    black icing 22
Frankentreat 116–17

G
ganache
    dark chocolate 13

  covering a cake with 19
glaze *see* apricot glaze
glue *see* tylose glue

H
hazelnut flavouring 16
Hero Time 30–3, 140–1 (t)
how to store 7
hundreds and thousands *see* nonpareil sugar balls
hygiene 7

I
Iced Bobo 106–7, 136 (t)
icing 12–15, 19, 20–3
  buttercream 13
  fondant 14–15
  dark chocolate ganache 13
  royal icing 14
  techniques 19–23
icing sugar 14
In Full Bloom 34–9, 139 (t)
It's a Goal 70–3, 137 (t)

K
knives, sharp and serrated 8, 9 *see also* palette knives

L
Laced Up 48–51, 138 (t)
layering technique for cakes 19, *19*
leaf cutter 8, 9
leaf veiner 8, 9
levelling cakes 19, *19*
levelling cupcakes 21
lining tins 17
lollies (as decorations) 10, 11
Love Heart Birds 134–5, 137 (t)
lustres *see* edible lustres

M
mocha flavouring 16
modelling pastes 14
modelling tools *8*, 9

Musical Silhouette 34–5, 138 (t)

N
nonpareil sugar balls 10, 11
non-stick baking paper 17
non-stick baking spray 17
Not So Cute Cupcakes 112–17

O
Oh! Babushka 108–11

P
paintbrushes 8, 9
palette knives 8, 9
Perfect Fit 56–9, 141 (t)
petal dusts 10, 11
Petit Tiered Cakes 40–3
piping techniques 14, 23
  dots and spots 23
  lines and writing 23
  teardrops 23
piping tips 8, 9
planning and organisation 6–7
preparing tins and trays 17
problems
  cakes too soft 7
  fondant too soft 22, 23
  icing too runny 22
Puppy Love 104–7, 136 (t)

Q
Queen Cachous
Queen Icing Flowers 10, 11

R
raspberry flavouring 16
rolling pins 8, 9
royal icing 14, 22–3
  colouring 22, *22*
  for biscuits 22
rum and raisin flavouring 16
RTR (Ready-to-Roll) icing *see* Bakels Pettinice RTR Icing, fondant icing

S
scissors 8, 9
scraper, straight-edged 8, 9, 19
Setting Sail 74–7, 136 (t)
sieve, super-fine 14
smoothers (for icing) 9, 20
So Chic 52–5, 136 (t)
sprinkles *see* nonpareil sugar balls
stitching tool *8*, 9
storage of cakes 7
storage of fondant 14
sugar confetti 10, 11
Sugar Suki 106–7, 136 (t)
supports for cakes, various 8, 9
Sweets for the Sweet 78–82

T
Teatale Party 60–4
timeframe for decoration 6–7
tins, cake 17
trays for cupcakes 17
turntable 8, 9
Tuxedos and Tiaras 26–9, 137 (t)
tylose powder 15

V
Vanilla Bean Birdhouse 130–5
vanilla bean biscuits 18

W
Welcome Bundle 124–9, 140 (t)
We'll Always Have Paris 96–9, 137 (t)
white chocolate & vanilla cake or cupcakes 16
white hand towels 7
Wonderful Time, A 66–9
work board, non-stick 8, 9
workspace requirements 7

Y
Yummy Mummy 114–15

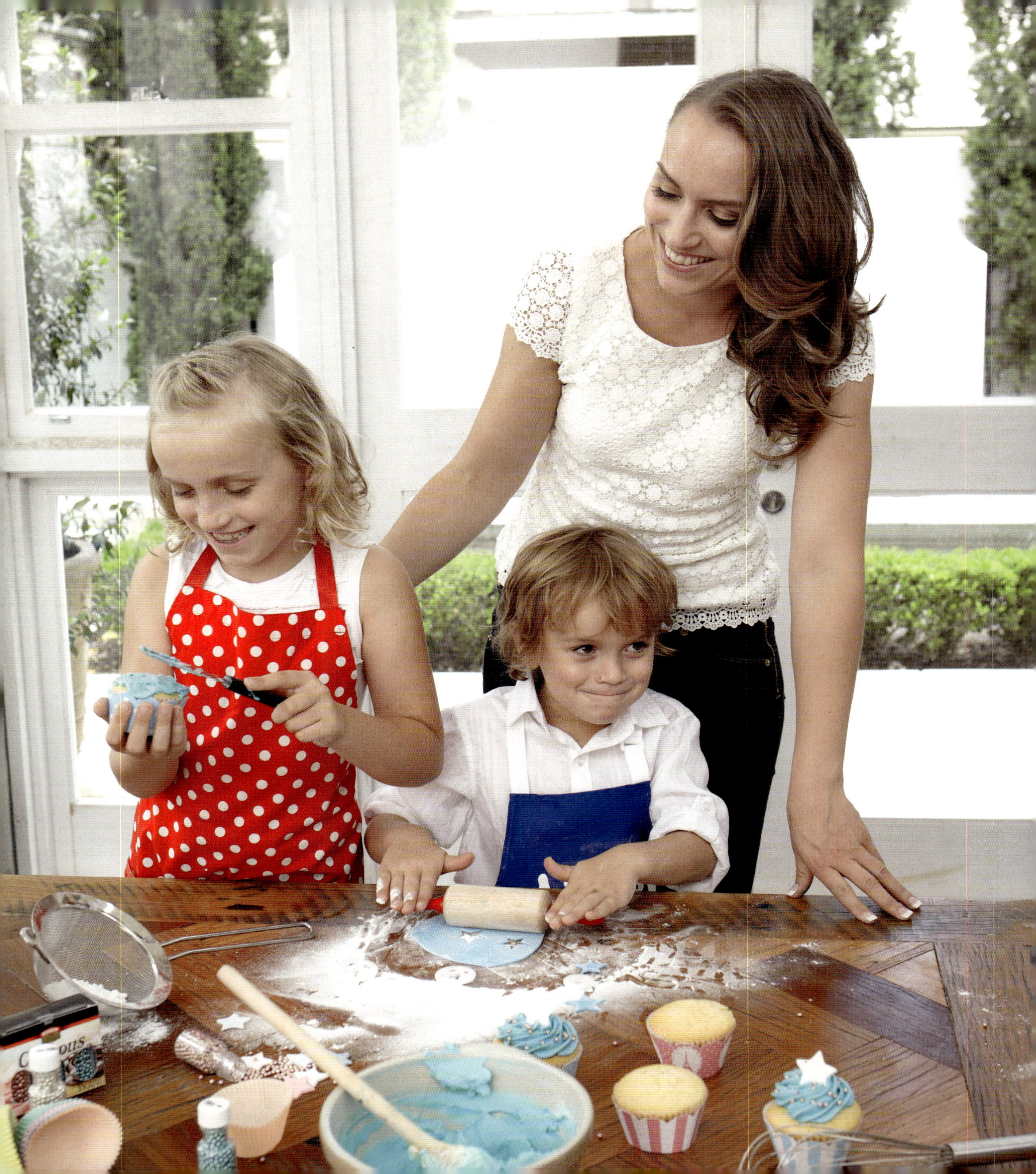